We **Call** *Him* "Coach"

Four Decades of Memories with Coach Dick McDonald

D1528665

Marcy McDonald-Bialeschki

Wasteland Press

www.wastelandpress.net
Shelbyville, KY USA

We Call Him "Coach":
Four Decades of Memories with Coach Dick McDonald
by Marcy McDonald-Bialeschki

First Printing – October 2012
ISBN: 978-1-60047-790-4

Printed in the U.S.A.

0   1   2   3   4   5   6   7   8   9   10   11   12

For My Daddy,
Coach Dick McDonald

Love you,

Leda

Table of Contents

Introduction

My dad is a completely ordinary yet utterly amazing man who turned a small town in central Illinois into a sports hot-spot for the better part of 4 decades. If you lived anywhere near Blue Mound, Illinois, in the 1970's, you have most likely heard of the Blue Mound Knights and Coach Dick McDonald.

When my dad retired from teaching and coaching, he could not just *stop* being a coach and educator. True, he was not physically coaching anymore, but he still had the mind of a strategist, and he had memories - many, many memories. For decades he carried folded pieces of notebook paper covered with meticulously scribed highlights of his vast career. A wealth of other tidbits remained in his mind, and these facts would often leak out as *stories* in casual conversation. He would tell people about his teams and his players and their phenomenal achievements, and I would say to him, "Daddy, you really need to write this all down."

In the winter of 2012 he finally began the arduous process of researching his own career. While he knew many years, events, times, and details, he did have some blanks. He began filling those blanks by searching through his personal records which included boxes of memorabilia he had collected over the decades. For further assistance, he looked to the local library and their collection of high school yearbooks to help him complete a statistical history of his teams and players.

The more my dad researched his vast career, the more he wanted to add. From about February 2012 through early fall, he researched regularly and gave me sections to type, and I continued to chronicle my personal memories and write some of his famous stories. The end result is this collection of facts and memories that piece together the decades of my father's career. I began this project as a way to preserve my dad's legacy as the Winningest Coach in the history of the Blue Mound Knights, but it has grown to be much more. The information here not only summarizes my dad's career but also preserves a piece of Blue Mound Knights sports history.

At the thought of publishing our labors, my dad's biggest fear was that some information would be incomplete or incorrect and consequently offend someone. If there was any doubt about the accuracy of information, every effort was made to verify the dubious details. In the end, we both felt we had a document that was as complete and as accurate as we could get it.

Thank you to all who contributed and to all who have been a part of my dad's incredible life. I can honestly say I have completed this project for my dad, but he has completed it for all of his athletes. So, in honor of my dad, his incredible legacy with the Blue Mound Knights, and all of his athletes over the years, I present: *We Call Him "Coach": Four Decades of Memories with Coach Dick McDonald.*

-Marcy McDonald-Bialeschki

The Fundamentals

- "Portrait of a Coach Then and Now"

- "Being a Knight"

- "An Inside Look at all those (K)Nights in the Gym"

- "Flat and Fast"

- "Formidable Foe: Mt. Pulaski Hilltoppers"

- "What's in a Name"

"Portrait of a Coach: Then and Now"

My dad has a Masters' degree in psychology, and I have always said this makes him a Master Motivator. More than anyone I have ever known, he understands what makes people "tick," and he has the uncanny ability to use what he knows about people to bring out the best in them. When he was teaching and coaching, he used this skill everyday to inspire and motivate his students and athletes. Sometimes bringing out the best in people means altering their behavior. Those of us who have been in a classroom with my dad know there is a certain *look* he reserves to show his extreme disapproval. I think all who have been the target of this look can agree that it does far more damage than even the most extreme verbal reprimand, and it is definitely capable of changing negative behavior.

When Janice Beck-Weathers (Class of 1976) mentioned her experience with *the look,* I had to chronicle it here. I believe Janice's experience can represent all similar experiences for the hundreds who know the power *the look* holds. But before I get to Janice's story, I also feel compelled to express that the one standard my dad holds in the highest regard is sportsmanship. This fact is essential to understanding the full significance of Janice's story.

My dad built his coaching philosophy on the tenets of good sportsmanship. Athletes were taught to respect themselves and to respect authority. They were taught to own up to their mistakes and never make excuses. The athlete who was charged with a foul in a basketball game accepted that call and raised his hand even after the rule was changed and players were no longer required to do so. That player did not argue with the officials or incite the fans with gestures and facial expressions. He took full responsibility for that call whether he felt it was justified or not. The player who did not follow these rules found himself sitting the bench and dreading his post game "conversation" with my dad. Don't get me wrong, there were plenty of times my dad felt the officials made a poor call, but that was his fight, not the player's. Additionally, a player was not allowed to look a referee in the eyes or speak to him because his authority had to be respected. There were no theatrics on the court, just good basketball. The Blue Mound Knights played every game with class, and this approach made winning look effortless.

My dad expected this same level of sportsmanship from his fans as well. If you were not a good sport, you were not a good fan. This is where we get back to Janice's story. She sent me a message on Facebook after hearing that I was helping my dad write his memoirs. These are her words:

I also remember one time at a basketball game ... I don't remember who we were playing but I think it was either Warrensburg or Macon...anyway....the refs had been making bad calls the entire game. I got so frustrated that I offered the referee my eyeglasses and your Dad stood up from the bench and just looked at me ... in the way that he could....and I sat down on the bleachers and didn't offer my glasses again. It wasn't so funny at the time but looking back I can only imagine what he was thinking.

Above all, my dad was an educator. He worked hard to teach students that good sportsmanship is an attribute that is necessary for success in everyday life. I was not surprised at all to read that my dad, in the middle of a tough game, was providing crowd control from across the gymnasium. Janice got *the look*, and it was effective. She got caught up in the energy of the game and lost her self-control for a moment, and my dad...with his *look*....taught her a little lesson in sportsmanship and what it meant to be a fan of the Blue Mound Knights. As it turned out, that lesson has stayed with her.

Over the years, there were plenty of times when my dad's sportsmanship was challenged. There was the time a coach dumped the water from all of his team's water bottles onto the court and the time that same coach simulated the act of mooning my dad and his players as they were heading to the locker room. There were the instances when entire cheering sections from the opposing team would stand up and sing "Old MacDonald" in the middle of a game. There were times when other players and coaches refused to shake my dad's hand or the hands of his players. He was spit on, shoved, puked on, and yelled at....the list goes on and on. Even though these actions infuriated my dad, he never let it show. His response was more sophisticated. He used these actions by other coaches, fans, and teams to motivate his players, and he just kept reinforcing the fact that winning, and losing, with dignity is the mark of a true winner.

Even though his days of teaching and coaching are behind him, my dad has not lost his gift of communication, and he has not lost his conviction for sportsmanship. In most ways he is the same, just a little older and grayer. Those who knew him then and still know him today would agree that his principles and beliefs have not wavered. My dad, the Master Motivator, can still talk his way around people, and when words are not possible or maybe not even necessary, he can still fire off *the look*. I know this because even though I am now in my 40's, I still occasionally get *the look*, and I have no trouble understanding its message.

The Look is captured here in a time out photo that appeared in the *Decatur Herald and Review* in 1977. Coach looks to David Scales to get the job done. Seated on the bench L to R: Mike Jackson, Kelly Armstrong, David Scales, and Brad Eckols.

"Being a Knight"

In Blue Mound during the Coach McDonald years, the basketball *team* was made up of more than just its players. My dad considered every interested participant to be part of the game-plan. The players, the cheerleaders, the statisticians, and the fans all had vital roles in Blue Mound's success. Since all of these components were indispensable to my dad, he treated them all as *players*. Likewise, he expected these participants to uphold his high standards of behavior and sportsmanship. It was tough work being a Blue Mound Knight, but the payoffs were extraordinary.

My dad was always very particular about his players' appearance because appearance factored into that air of class and good sportsmanship he values so highly. Back in the 70's my dad didn't care that short hair was not *cool*. He required his players to be clean-cut and have short haircuts because he had an image he wanted to portray. He also required players to wear their varsity sport coats back in the 60's and 70's and required them to wear dress pants and nice shirts or sweaters in the 80's and 90's. They always sat as a team and watched the junior varsity game, and there was no horsing around and no contact with girlfriends because appearance was important. When the buzzer rang to end the 3rd quarter, they all left as a team to prepare for the varsity game, and the entire Blue Mound cheering section stood and clapped as a show of support. As a fan in my childhood days and then as a cheerleader in high school, I felt extremely proud when the players left the gym as a group because they were clean-cut, well dressed and they held their heads high because they were Blue Mound Knights.

A real Knight also had to have his "head in the game." Players were expected to act as if every day was game day. My dad expected players to look, act, and think like winners every minute of every day. While there was room in a player's life for other activities such as friends and girlfriends, when it looked as if these outside elements were causing a problem, my dad was liable to step in. This is exactly what happened to Renee Damery-Bailey. Here are her words:

Hey Marcy, I have a memory about your Dad. I had been dating Ed [Bailey] for a couple years and then we broke up for awhile and I started dating Tim Rainey. One day after Ed and I broke up, your Dad called me into his office. I was so scared. I don't remember exactly what he said but he pretty much told me that he didn't want me messing with his basketball players heads and getting their game off. Ha ha!

I love the way Renee added the "ha ha" to the end of this message. I'm sure at the time she was not able to laugh, but she is now. As with the message I received from Janice Beck-Weathers, I was not at all surprised when I read Renee's words. For the record, Renee was a cheerleader all 4 four years of high school from 1974 to 1978. She was part of the powerhouse era of the 1970's when the Blue Mound Knights went on a 42 game conference winning streak. In fact, the incident she wrote about probably occurred during the middle of that streak and in the middle of the only undefeated regular season in the history of the Blue Mound Knights. The guys she mentions in her note were both starters. It appears as if my dad was running a little interference to prevent any possible chinks in the armor. From the sound of her words, I am fairly sure Renee got the message.

Aside from his actual players, my dad liked to make sure the other people in the inner circle of the program were as steadfast as he when it came to sportsmanship and appearance. I'm not really sure, but I think my dad was the first coach in our area to have high school girls keep stats for him. He hand-picked his statisticians based on their dependability, their neat handwriting, and their ability to keep their composure in the heat of a challenging game. Once chosen, his statisticians were fondly referred to as "His Girls." Renee Sperry-Trimble (Class of 1977) mentioned that she felt like such a special part of the team being a statistician. "I remember being chosen. And after you are chosen to be one of "His Girls," you just feel like you are on top of the world," said Renee who later ended up working with my dad in the high school office for many years.

Part of this special feeling came from the fact that the statisticians wore distinct varsity sweaters that identified them as a group and made them a unique part of the basketball program. Aside from keeping meticulous records, many times the statisticians were asked to protect my dad and his players. Sitting behind the players' bench, over in enemy territory, they would often stand during timeouts to shield my dad and the team from the menacing words and glares of the opposing fans. These girls would sometimes get yelled at and cursed, but they held their ground with stoic resolve. This was part of their job, and they performed perfectly at every game. In fact, most of the statistics in this book originated from their labors. It is obvious that they were a valued part of the team every year.

Cheerleaders were another valued component of the team. Many coaches do not fully appreciate the contributions cheerleaders make to the team effort, but my dad knew cheerleaders were instrumental to his overall purpose. A cheerleader for the Blue Mound Knights assumed the awesome responsibility of promoting, supporting, and inspiring her team. A cheerleader for the Knights also had to energize as well as control the fans. Cheerleaders arrived to games in uniform, and they sat as a group if they were not cheering. They *definitely* did not mingle with the players. As with the statisticians, my dad had a hand in choosing his cheerleaders. The only years he did not judge tryouts were the years I was in high school. My dad treated his cheerleaders with respect, and in return he expected them to perform and behave in a manner appropriate for a Blue Mound Knight.

Through it all, my dad was our Coach and our mentor, and being a part of his team was a special calling. True, it was a tremendous responsibility, yet it was also extremely rewarding. Through the good times, as well as the not so good times, the players, statisticians, cheerleaders, and fans functioned as a team, and it was our mission to honorably represent Coach McDonald, Blue Mound High School, and the Blue Mound Knights.

Although Coach was a serious competitor, he was also a grand jokester. He is pictured here with cheerleaders from left to right: Dani Meador, Rita Canaday, Julie Garrison and Renee Damery. It appears he is "causing trouble" in the background while their sponsor, Janet Damery, stands either unaware or unimpressed that her squad is being distracted.

"An Inside Look into all those (K)Nights in the Gym"

Over the 22 years my dad coached basketball, there were plenty of players who could provide "insider information" about the *real* course of events at a Blue Mound Knights basketball practice; however, many of them might not have realized that their practices were somewhat out of the ordinary compared to the practices of their competitors. The main difference was the fact that my dad was passionate about practicing *skills* and less interested in playing an actual game. For that reason, he hardly ever ran scrimmage drills or played intra-squad games. According to my dad, most of his practices were broken down into 4 sets of *skills*: passing drills for the half-court offense and fast break; free throw shooting as a team with game pressure; special defensive situations such as the 1 – 2 – 2 match up, defending the last shot, and presses; and special offensive situations such as shooting a last second shot and the "trash." These skills and situations were practiced regularly, but they were not the only *constant* of the practices. Another general custom involved strengthening and testing the players' discipline and patience.

Blue Mound High School dismissed every day at 3:36:30 pm. As a teacher, counselor, athletic director, and dean of students, my dad was rarely able to arrive at the gymnasium for practice right after the dismissal bell; however, the players were expected to head directly to the locker room, get dressed, grab a basketball, and sit on the bench until he walked in the gymnasium, which was always right around 4:00 pm. No one was up walking, talking, dribbling, shooting.......*nothing* until their coach entered.

My dad recalled one instance when a Marine recruiter was visiting in the office and stayed awhile after school. Finally, after about 20 minutes, my dad told him he needed to be heading down to the gym for practice. The recruiter followed him down to the lobby and before they said their goodbyes, my dad asked him to look inside the doors and tell him what was going on. The Marine opened the door, looked in and saw about 30 boys sitting on the bench holding basketballs. He closed the door, looked at my dad and said, "Have you ever been a Marine?" The answer, of course, was, "no," but the connection was accurate. The relationship between my dad and his players was one of respect, trust, and discipline. My dad knew before he asked the recruiter to open the door, that all of his players would be sitting on the bench because that was the routine.

Once my dad arrived at practice, the routine continued with a passing drill. The varsity would run 3 lanes, make 2 or 3 passes and finish with a jump shot at the end. A triangle defense would challenge the shooter, and "made" shots were counted for the team. After the passing drill, players would practice field goals. Eight shooters would shoot 100 shots as a team, one at a time from their offensive position. They rotated from one player to the next with all players shooting 12 shots and 4 would have to shoot an extra shot for a total of 100. This drill was repeated until an acceptable amount of shots were made.

The next part of the routine would consist of shooting free throws. It's no secret that free throws can win basketball games, and every time a Blue Mound Knight went to the line, he felt confident because he had shot free throws under pressure at practice every night. Teams of 8 players would line up at the free throw line as they would in a game. Each team would shoot 3 rotations and then choose who would shoot the last shot. At least 20 baskets of the 25 shots had to be made or they ran 17 sprints down the length of the gym floor. After the sprints, the drill would begin again. On occasion, practices ran long because the obligatory 80% had not been achieved. This drill was designed to simulate game pressure shooting, and it worked.

My dad remembers one time when the Knights were down by one point and one of his players went to the line shooting a one-on-one with 3 seconds on the clock. The player made both shots and the Knights won the game. After the game a newspaper reporter interviewed the player and asked him how he was able to overcome the pressure. My dad remembers the player answering by saying that the game pressure was not nearly as bad as the pressure to make free throws during practice. It seems like the time spent on practicing free throws was time well spent.

Offense and defense were also practiced regularly as well as shooting technique. All of this practice developed – in many cases - unmatched skills. My dad takes a lot of pride in the shooting reputation his teams earned. He loved hearing others share their thoughts on his teams, especially when they were explaining Blue Mound basketball to people who weren't familiar with their habits. Scouts would report on "great shooters," and explain that fouling was not a good strategy since that exceptional shooting ability applied to the line as well. Another piece of advice for novice teams would always include the necessity to "get back" on defense because they would "run on every play."

One of the funniest scouting reports my dad ever heard about his teams was relayed to him at a coaches' meeting. One of the coaches - when trying to describe the Blue Mound Fast Break - shared that it had been named "Zip, Zip, Yeah!" When one of the newer coaches of the group looked a little bewildered he explained, "Yeah, it's just 2 passes and a score." This kind of notoriety and consistency became the standard for Blue Mound basketball, and it all went back to the meticulously orchestrated practices.

From beginning to end, my dad's basketball practices were planned, productive, and very, very routine. Some nights things went more smoothly than others, but overall I think the outcome speaks for itself.

Pictured here in a familiar pose, Coach McDonald evaluates a pre-game warm up.

"Flat and Fast"

For many years, Blue Mound basketball players lacked the conditioning a fall sport could provide. To alleviate this issue, Coach McDonald looked to cross country to get his players in shape and ready to run up and down the court in November. Therefore, in 1971 cross country was adopted by the school board, and Coach McDonald created a flat and fast course designed to run through the village and come to its end on school property, with a total of 2.95 miles covered.

It's true that cross country's beginnings sprung from a need for basketball players to get in shape, but this fact soon became just a bonus for McDonald and his teams. McDonald's competitive spirit and predilection for winning gave cross country its own identity, and just as in any other sport, Blue Mound became a fiery competitor. But success doesn't just happen. There has to be talent and motivation and strategy. Therefore, McDonald, the strategist, devised a practice that challenged each runner to perform at his personal best, regardless of his talent. This strategy didn't have a special name, but it became a team favorite year after year.

McDonald would gather the stats from previous races and list each runner's best time on the home course from slowest to fastest. The difference in times would be the "advantage" for the slower runners. The slowest runner would take off first and the next slowest runner would follow, after the difference of their times had passed. All runners would do the same, with the fastest runner taking off last. The objectives are somewhat obvious: The slower runners in the front of the pack were trying to keep other runners from catching them, and the faster runners were pushing themselves to catch the ones who had gotten ahead of them. The nature of this practice put runners in course positions they ordinarily didn't have and made them adjust their running to the situation. Faster runners were not used to being behind. They would generally run their fastest times during this practice because they had to "catch up." Likewise, slower runners were in the unusual position of maintaining a lead, so they often had better times during this practice as well. Mathematically, all runners should have finished at the same time, but this never happened because each runner – being out of his element – was running a very different race.

Because cross country was essentially the conditioning for basketball, everyone who wanted to play basketball was expected to be on the team. Therefore, the overall team usually consisted of 25 to 30 runners. At home meets all of these team members ran, but larger meets only allowed a team of 7 to compete. While the top 7 runners received most of the accolades from year to year, Coach McDonald knew a runner didn't have to be in the top 7 to benefit from the sport. Runners were dedicated to practices and home meets and ran to try to beat their personal best times; therefore, a participant didn't have to be in the top 7 to earn a varsity letter. True, much of the time the spotlight was on the traveling team, but every runner was valued and pushed to achieve at his own level.

After all the running out on the course was over for a year, those same guys hit the hardwood. While many of them may not have enjoyed running cross country in the fall, they all had to agree that being in shape made enduring basketball practices much, much easier. Putting the time in on the flat and fast course outside proved to be an instrumental factor in Blue Mound basketball; however, McDonald would argue that over time, cross country proved to be another sport where his athletes could excel.

"Formidable Foe: Mt. Pulaski Hilltoppers"

1977...1978...1984...These are the years of some of the best basketball Blue Mound High School and Coach McDonald ever witnessed. These are also the years Blue Mound's post-season dreams were extinguished by Coach Ed Butkovich and the Mt. Pulaski Hilltoppers. It seems terribly coincidental that in 3 of the 7 times Blue Mound saw sectional play in Coach McDonald's career, further advancement into the post-season was denied by the same coach and the same team. While I am no expert on the career of Coach Ed Butkovich or his teams, I do know one thing: Beating Coach Dick McDonald and the Blue Mound Knights 3 times is a major accomplishment.

In 1977 Coach McDonald led the Knights to their first-ever undefeated regular season in school history. The Knights went on to win the Regional and the first round of the Shelbyville Sectional before facing the Hilltoppers of Mt. Pulaski. Coach McDonald and the Knights knew this game would be a struggle, especially since the Hilltoppers had earned a trip to the Big House the previous season and walked away as the State Champions. Back in 1991 Coach Butkovich was interviewed by *Decatur Herald and Review* sports reporter Jeff Lampe for a story about the final retirement of Coach McDonald. Like McDonald, Butkovich had a remarkable coaching career, but recalled the '76-'77 game against Blue Mound as, "one of the best games we've ever been involved with and probably one of the most exciting sectional games ever played (at Shelbyville)." Many people say this Sectional Final game between Blue Mound and Mt. Pulaski was, in fact, every bit as exciting as a State Championship game.

In the same interview by Lampke, Butkovich went on to say, "The thing I remember is going over to Dick with about two minutes left in the game and shaking his hand, putting my arm around him and saying, 'I don't know who is going to win this one but this has been one heck of a ballgame.'" When the final buzzer sounded, it was Butkovich's team that would advance to the Super Sectional and ultimately go on to earn fourth place the High School Boys' Basketball State Tournament that year. A tough blow for the Knights, this loss ended a phenomenal and historical season. Looking back, Coach McDonald, like Butkovich, sees his '76-'77 team as "something special." McDonald and his Knights and Butkovich were not finished doing battle, however. They met again in the very next season for another Sectional show-down at Shelbyville.

Once again in 1978, the Knights squared off against the Hilltoppers from Mt. Pulaski, and once again Coach McDonald came face to face with the only man who could say he had beaten the Knights the previous year. This game, like the first, was an incredible battle to the finish. In the end, the Hilltoppers were once again victorious. A final score of 80 – 63 does not quite illustrate the close battle that ensued for most of the game. Despite the loss, McDonald was eventually satisfied with the outcome, knowing his team played well, and that they had been defeated by a formidable foe, worthy of the accomplishment. However, it did sting that dreams of advancing to the State Tournament had been crushed once again. At this point, McDonald's relationship with Coach Butkovich was one built on mutual respect. While McDonald didn't like to lose, he respected Butkovich and his team, and after losing for the second time, he went on to root for the Hilltoppers who were beaten by Sullivan in the Super Sectional game.

After the end of the 1979-80 season, Coach McDonald focused on a few more winning seasons and then endured a few lean years. However, by the mid-1980's he was back to his old tricks. McDonald and the Knights won the Regional Tournament and advanced through the first game of the Sectional in the '82 – 83' season. After it was all over, McDonald sat back and counted his blessings that 3 of his starters and much of his bench would return. As he was cruising through a 26 – 1 regular season the next year ('83 – '84), McDonald had no way of knowing that he would once again face his nemesis from the north, Coach Ed Butkovich and his mighty Hilltoppers.

In early March of 1984, McDonald took his Knights to the Shelbyville Sectional Tournament one more time. Losing only 1 regular season game and claiming his 7th Regional Championship title, McDonald was ready to do battle with Butkovich once again. In Lampke's 1991 article in the *Decatur Herald and Review*, Butkovich remembered, "He [McDonald] was a fiery competitor and every time you faced his teams you knew they were going to give you a battle." He was right. I imagine Butkovich felt the odds were stacked against him. Beating Blue Mound twice is difficult; beating them 3 times would be nearly impossible. Sure enough, the 1984 battle was fought to the last second, but once again McDonald and his team had to surrender. Butkovich and his Hilltoppers had defeated the odds and would advance in the Sectional over the Knights and ultimately earn a 2nd place finish in the State Tournament.

This is quite a history between these two legendary coaches. Today, McDonald says he can remember every last detail of those games, and even though the final outcome for each game was not as favorable as it could have been, he sees those games as some of his best. I am sure if Coach Butkovich was still with us, he would say the same. Three years, three battles, three different teams, and two remarkable coaches: now that's high school boys' basketball at its best.

Ed Butkovich
... Mount Pulaski

This picture appeared in
the *Decatur Herald and Review*
in the mid 1970's.

This story is dedicated to Coach Ed Butkovich who passed in 2002. Thanks for the memories.

"What's in a Name?"

We've all heard the saying, "What's in a name?" Well, apparently, to my dad, a great deal. Recently, I received this message from Janice Beck-Weathers which reminded me that one of my dad's great talents – other than coaching – was inventing nicknames for people.

"Marcy....I know that you are helping your Dad. I remember your Dad as always having a nickname for everyone. It was pretty cool that once you got a nickname from him ... that name stuck!"

Janice is right. My dad had a nickname for almost everyone. My dad's nicknames were his way of showing a student or athlete that he or she was special. The nickname was descriptive, genuine, unique, and maybe even a bit embarrassing initially. But the nickname was also a personal acknowledgement from my dad that he was invested in you – that he *knew* you, and that you mattered. As Janice stated, it was "pretty cool" when you got your nickname. From that moment in time, you assumed that identity, and friends, teachers, even family members knew you as this new alias.

Janice's comments motivated me to talk with my dad and to inspire him to search his memory for as many nicknames as he could recall. This turned out to be a monumental task for a man who had a nickname for students and athletes covering four decades. At some point, my dad decided he would concentrate only on athletes, and even then he worried he would leave someone out. Apologies go out to any who are not chronicled here. My dad wanted to add that nearly every athlete was most often referred to by his last name during "serious times" and the nicknames listed below were the more comical, light-hearted names my dad became known for. Again, please do not be offended if you are omitted.

NICKNAME	ATHLETE
Bug Hunter	Mike Bourisaw
Hoyt	Mike Wilhoit
Pearl	Bruce Bailey
Oaf	Matt Sefried
Younk	Tom Younker
Spoon	Brad Eckols
Rang	John Pistorius
Stork	Jeff Brown
Slick	Rick Brown
Bear	Jim Brown
Nick	Tod Nicholls
Big Red	Gene Giles
Darius	Dan Hutton
Huff	Ken Huffman
Bobcat	Brent Damery
Jaybird	Jay Brown
Brownie	Kim Brown
Pistol	Dave Pistorius
Big Hoss	Dave Pistorius
Jack	Gary Jackson
"14"	Gary Jackson
Little Jack	Mike Jackson
Little Danny	Danny Byard
Pokie	Todd Logue
Loguer	Todd Logue
Hoke	Jerry Logue
Pretty Boy	Steve Williams
Billy	Bill Younker
Pedro	Pete Gilson
Jewser	Scott Jewsbury
Took	Chris Scott
Wildman	George Booker
Kamikaze	Randy Damery
Delmar	Doug Collier
Herman	Paul Sperry
Phileep	Phil Brown
Eagle Beak	Chuck Plunkett
Duck	Don Naber

Taxi	Gene Pistorius
Slamin' Sammy	Sam Pate
Buckey	Mark Davis
Zebco	Leon Zeeb
Jeep	Jeff Zeeb
Steino	Stein Villumstad
Hammer	Ken Ervin
Beaver	Kevin Burns
Fitz	Doug Fitzgerald
Pit	Tim Armstrong
House	Mark Houser
Wooley	Doug Woolever
Doc	Doug Mathias
Slavian	Mladen Matisa
Jose	Joe Zeeb
Fitz	Dan Fitzgerald

A Glimpse at a Lifetime of Stories

- "That's My Boy"

- "The Great Communicator"

- "Have a Little Faith"

- "Sir, We are a Team. End of Discussion"

- "Win…That's What They Do"

- "My Girl Is Never Wrong"

- "It's Not Whether You Win or Lose – It's How You Play the Game"

- "Keep Your Eyes on the Ball"

- "The Wife Speaks"

The stories in this section are some of my dad's all-time favorites. I have done my best to put them in print and portray them as accurately as I can. Please remember, these are stories originating from several decades ago. I apologize if they do not match others' memories from the past, but I have made careful attempts to present them as I remember my dad telling them.

"That's *My* Boy!"

The people who know my dad best know he loves to tell stories, and in these stories he has a tendency to brag. He is not, however, the typical braggart. His accolades most often honor his athletes and not himself because most great coaches know that their abilities have limits. While a great coach can nurture and develop an athlete's talent, he also knows a certain level of athleticism must first exist inherently. Since leaving coaching, one of my dad's favorite pastimes is bragging about his athletes' success. Back in the day, however, he would not have dreamt of bragging, at least not until the competition was over. There was always an heir of mystery about my dad in that way. He was definitely a contradiction of terms. He was confident and proud, yet an underlying current of humility ran in his veins. He always considered bragging "in the moment" to be poor sportsmanship, not to mention bad strategy.

This confident humility can best be illustrated by his experience at the Effingham Invitational Cross Country meet in the fall of 1978. That was the year his star runner, Mike Jackson, was a senior. Mike was truly a standout runner, not only for Blue Mound fans, but he was also recognized as a top runner in the area and in the state. For the record, the rest of the team that year was pretty good as well, but Mike was definitely expected to finish at the front of the pack with his teammates not far behind.

Small town schools like Blue Mound are always underdogs in large Invitationals. The Effingham Invitational hosted schools from all over central and southern Illinois. The size of the school didn't matter. There were teams from large towns like Charleston, Effingham, Champaign and more. Likewise, good runners and teams from smaller schools could attend if they felt they could "run with the big dogs," so to speak. The thing about those larger schools - they often completely underestimated schools like Blue Mound and runners like Mike Jackson. Of course, most coaches did their research, and in 1978, most coaches did, in fact, know Mike Jackson. But there was one coach from East Saint Louis who had no knowledge of Blue Mound High School, Coach McDonald or Mike Jackson. And he had no idea what he was in for that day.

Just prior to the start of the meet, my dad had befriended the coach of the East Saint Louis Fliers. This fast friendship could not have been made between two more opposite men. The coach of the Fliers was dressed in a flashy track suit accessorized with gold chains. He wore a fancy wristwatch that he also used as a stopwatch. He was loud and overly confident, and he could not stop talking about his star runner who he affectionately referred to as Jivin' Jimmy. My dad, I'm fairly certain, wore blue jeans, Red Wing boots, and a Blue Mound Knights hat. He probably also wore a blue windbreaker and used Ray Bands to conceal his "game face" when necessary. When the Fliers' coach was going on and on about "his boy," my dad was quietly sizing up Mike's competition. Not long after the start gun sounded, the boisterous coach asked my dad if he wanted to ride to the mile check point in his golf cart. Finding the conversation a bit humorous, my dad got in the cart and headed to the mile marker with his talkative companion.

When they arrived at the mile marker, the Fliers' coach moved with a great gesture to check the elaborate stopwatch mounted on his wrist.

"My boy ought to be coming around that corner about now," he boasted. "He hasn't been beaten all year."

My dad recalled hearing that statement – "My boy hasn't been beaten all year" – more than a few times on his cart ride to the check point. It was probably pretty hard for him to refrain from mentioning a few facts and statistics about his own *boy,* but he did. While my dad had all the confidence in the world in Mike, he didn't know this other runner. So when the first runner emerged from the woods, he was more than a little relieved it was *his boy.* In a complete state of confusion, his cart-buddy bellowed, "That's not my boy!" To this declaration my dad – with a grin - replied, "I know. That's *my* boy."

The Fliers' coach was dumbfounded. A little more guarded now, he headed the cart to the second mile check point. This check point was laid out much like the first one, where the runners emerged from around a wooded corner, so the leader was a well-kept secret through most of the second mile leg of the race. In the course of just a few minutes, the atmosphere in the cart had drastically changed. The once boastfully confident big city coach suddenly seemed insecure, quiet, and maybe a little embarrassed. The anticipation of not knowing who would emerge from the woods was excruciating for Jivin' Jimmy's mentor. My dad was secretly enjoying his pain and feeling a little vindicated for having to endure the prideful boasts of Jimmy's greatness. The big city coach checked his watch and scoured the edge of the woods, fearing the outcome. Once again, the leader of the pack came thundering out of the woods, and it was *not* Jivin' Jimmy.

"Damn, your boy is good! Can he finish?"

This question and its naïve origin amused my dad, "Yep."

By this time Jimmy had cleared the woods and his coach was yelling, "You catch him, Jimmy. He's a finisher! You catch him!! He's for real!!!"

And they were off to the finish line. There was no doubt in my dad's mind who would win. The best part of Mike's race was always the last leg. If Jivin' Jimmy hadn't closed the gap by now, he wasn't going to. Yet his coach remained optimistic.

"My boy hasn't been beaten all year. He's gonna finish strong." He sounded convincing, almost too convincing, like he was trying to convince even himself.

Unlike the 1st and 2nd mile markers, the finish line was a long, visible stretch and by this time the spectators could see the race leader in his final kick. It was Mike, and he had stretched the lead on his competition. The Fliers' coach was livid. "Come on, Jimmy!!! Catch him!!! Catch him!!!" But his rants were in vain. Jimmy was too far back and Mike's final kick was too strong. As Mike crossed the finish line in record time, my dad turned to Jimmy's coach and matter-of-factly said what he had been dying to say all morning long, " That's my boy! He hasn't been beaten all year."

At age 15, Mike Jackson finishes 1ˢᵗ in the District cross country meet at Kiwanis Park in Decatur, IL. Ferrell Flatt, superintendent at Niantic-Harristown HS and Gil Jones, Nianitc-Harristown's principal, keep the time. This picture is from the Decatur Herald and Review (Fall of 1976).

"The Great Communicator"

You've heard the saying: "You've gotta be able to *talk the talk* and *walk the walk*." Well, general consensus would have it that my dad, Coach Dick McDonald, can do just that. He tells it like it is and stands behind it, and if he makes a mistake, he owns up to it. Talking and motivating and communicating are an art form for my dad. For this reason, I guess you could call him The Great Communicator. But I remember one time when communication was lacking, and it almost cost the Blue Mound Knights a game.

When I was a sophomore in high school, we had an exchange student from Yugoslavia named Mladen. He was tall and athletically built, and I remember my dad sizing him up in the hallway, probably thinking of how he could be useful to the team. Come to find out, Mladen was quite the athlete, but he was a volleyball player and had never even touched a basketball. But my dad always said, "An athlete is an athlete." He was determined to get Mladen to go out for the team.

Since we did not have boys' volleyball at Blue Mound, Mladen, the athlete, had no choice but to go out for basketball. My dad convinced him it would keep him in shape for volleyball when he returned home to Yugoslavia. The Great Communicator was convincing, naturally, and Mladen became a Blue Mound Knight.

At his first practice, my dad probably regretted what he had done when he assessed Mladen's ball handling skills, which were *none*, by the way. He couldn't dribble, he didn't know any of the rules of the game, and he certainly couldn't shoot. Mladen could, however, jump, and somehow my dad knew he was a valuable work-in- progress. Sure enough, as time passed, the athlete in Mladen emerged, and he began to understand the basic rules of the game. By the time games started, Mladen was by no means a star player, but he wasn't awful either. He would sit by my dad on the bench, and my dad would explain the game as it was being played. Mladen was smart, and the Great Communicator was a good teacher. And even though English was Mladen's second language, he seemed to be learning more and more of the language every day. As a result, by the end of the season, he was getting a little "play" time.

At one particular game very late in the season, the Knights found themselves in a close match with just minutes to play. Now, this is not the usual time for Mladen to go in, but the Knights were having trouble rebounding the ball. Knowing Mladen had probably the best vertical jump of anyone on the team, my dad decided to take a chance and put him in the game.

Mladen had strict orders to jump straight up and grab the ball. If it was an offensive board, he could put it back up to score. This was a drill Mladen and my dad had worked on over and over, so they were both fairly confident, if given the chance, he could perform. On the defensive side of the court, things were a little more complicated. Jumping up and rebounding the ball was no problem. Knowing what to do with it next would be the challenging part. You see, while Mladen's skills had drastically improved, he still could not dribble, so "moving the ball" was out of the question. At this point my dad decided "getting the ball" was the most important thing, so Mladen entered the game.

In the Knights' first possession, much like it was rehearsed, Mladen jumped up and grabbed the ball, towering over the other players. His excitement and power probably startled a few, even ones from his own team. Once in possession of the ball, Mladen did what he had practiced hundreds of times. He put it back up on the backboard and watched it fall in the net. The crowd went crazy. Mladen didn't get a lot of play-time but when he did, he was a crowd favorite. My dad was pleased and not surprised that Mladen had delivered. But now the players were headed to the other end of the court, and once again Mladen was instructed to get the ball. So once again he jumped up and ripped the ball out of midair. Once his feet were planted on the floor he must have gotten caught up in the excitement of it all because instead of passing, he proceeded to move the ball down the floor. At first we all had high hopes that Mladen could maneuver out of this tough situation, but it wasn't long until his lack of ball handling skills was painfully obvious. When it was obvious that disaster was eminent, my dad started yelling, "Whoa!! Whoa!! Whoa!!" Unfortunately, in all of the excitement, Mladen was incited to finish what he had started. He continued his awkward path to the other end until he was called for traveling.

I vividly remember the response of the entire crowd. It was as if the gymnasium itself groaned in agony. And then, we all looked to the bench, fearing my dad's response. You guessed it. It was not pretty. As Mladen headed to the bench, my dad pointed to the end and told him, "You sit down there. You won't do what I say. Go sit at the end of the bench." Well, this exile must have been excruciating for Mladen because he slowly crept his way down the bench, moving player after player until he made it to the seat next to my dad. My dad remembers he sat there for quite awhile before mustering up enough courage to tap him on the shoulder.

"I told you to sit at the end of the bench, Mladen. You didn't follow my directions," my dad barked.

Mladen looked completely confused and decided to remain quiet for just a little longer. When there was a break in the action, he decided he would have another go at talking with his coach. So once again, Mladen tapped my dad on the shoulder. "Coach, I have just one question," Mladen said with trepidation.

My dad, getting completely annoyed, decided he had no choice but to deal with this problem right then and there. "Couldn't you hear me? Couldn't you hear me?" my dad yelled. "When I say, 'Whoa', I mean 'Whoa'!" And then my dad had this way of ending his *one-sided conversations* with his signature words, "Do you understand me?" which was always completely rhetorical. But the rhetorical aspect for Mladen, who only spoke English as a second language, was lost.

"I have question," Mladen adamantly stated.

"What?" my dad barked.

"What does *Whoa* mean?"

The Great Communicator was speechless.

Mladen Matisa is pictured here from the 1982 yearbook.

"Have a Little Faith"

From the very beginning of his career, my grandparents were steadfast supporters of my dad's teams. After all, they had endured countless games and practices while my dad was home playing ball from a very early age up through high school. They knew of my dad's athletic ability and love of the game(s), but even more importantly, they knew of his indelible competitive spirit. Win or lose - any game my dad played or coached would be a thrill to watch.

For these reasons, my grandpa held a season ticket and came to every home basketball game until he passed away in August of 1980. My grandma's arthritis prevented her from attending games, but she never missed a radio broadcast of a tournament game or a high profile conference match-up. Not long before my grandpa died, he and my grandma sold their farm house near Mt. Zion and moved to Blue Mound. After his death, living in Blue Mound was easier, safer, and a lot less lonely for my grandma.

Because she no longer had my grandpa to tell her all about the games, my dad got in the habit of going over to her house after games and telling her how they went. In 1984 the Knights were experiencing an especially good season. They went 26 – 2 for the year, and my grandma was delighted. One night she was listening to a game being broadcast on the radio – probably the Macon County Tournament. Anyway, the Knights were favored to win, and this type of pressure always made things a little *edgy*. The game this particular night was extremely close, and my grandma turned the radio off and back on several times. She wanted to know what was going on, but she just couldn't handle it when the Knights seemed to struggle. When it came down to the final minutes of the game, the opponents were ahead by 5 or 6 points and had possession of the ball. That was it! My grandma, extremely frustrated, turned the radio off for a final time. She spent the rest of the evening reconciling with the idea that her son's team had been delivered their first loss of the season.

When my dad arrived, he went through the regular routine, not seeming too upset. There was silence at first because my grandma didn't really know what to say. Finally, she broke the silence by offering, "Tough game tonight, huh, son?" True, it was a tough game, but my grandma didn't know that after she turned off her radio, the Knights had regained possession of the ball, scored multiple times, and had held their opponents scoreless. My dad and his team had won the game in the final minutes.

"Oh, I don't know, Mom," he replied. "It turned out alright in the end."

My grandma looked bewildered. "What?"

"It was rough, but we pulled it out in the end," my dad confirmed.

"Well, son-of-a-bitch!" my grandma hollered. "I turned the radio off with 3 minutes to go. I thought you lost."

My dad just grinned at her and said, "You should know better than that, Mom. Have a little faith."

My grandma smiled and let out a big sigh of relief. "Well, that's definitely the last time I turn the radio off... no matter what's going on."

"Yeah, you missed the best part of the game," my dad offered with a grin. With the tension broken, my dad filled her in on the exciting final moments of the game, and she enjoyed his play by play details just as much as hearing them on the radio. However, I am fairly confident that she held true to her promise and didn't turn her radio off prematurely ever again.

My dad had a love of sports from a very early age,
and my grandparents always supported him. He is pictured
here outside his childhood home in rural Mt. Zion,
at about age 10

"Sir, We Are a Team. End of Discussion"

As an educator myself, I think a lot of my dad's success as a coach grew from his uncanny ability to motivate and inspire his athletes. That's what great educators and coaches do. They believe that every participant has something special to offer, and they and convince each athlete that his gifts make him unbeatable. With this approach to coaching, my dad could inspire average athletes to be extraordinary just by instilling confidence.

Back in the early 1970's my dad asked for and was granted permission to create a cross country team. He felt it was important for his basketball players to be in shape when they came to practice in November. What may have started as a casual endeavor, soon erupted into another powerhouse sport for Blue Mound. By the second year, McDonald's team was gaining respect and winning meets. After a couple of years, they were winning huge Invitationals.

In the sport of cross country there is a basic *team* and a team that competes at large meets and at the Invitational level. The latter consists of 7 runners who have the best times and who have been the most consistent in practice and smaller meets. Of these 7, the top 5 are used for team scoring. For my dad, once this elite team of 7 was chosen, the "pecking order" would fluctuate considerably. Some weeks the 2nd runner would drop to the 3rd runner and the 4th runner would improve, so putting this team into a sequential order based on ability would have been difficult for my dad to do. Could he have figured out an order? Sure, but he never wanted to *label* his runners. A runner labeled the 3rd man on the team, is going to own that title and possibly never aspire beyond that goal. My dad wanted all of his runners to be working hard and challenging themselves and putting pressure on each other, so he was very much against labeling them.

One year in the late 1970's Blue Mound's cross country team was winning large meets and Invitationals right and left, and a sports writer from a local paper called my dad and wanted to do a story on Blue Mound's top 2 runners. Along with the story, he wanted to take some pictures for the paper. My dad tried to explain to the writer that he didn't have 2 *top* runners, he had a *team*. The writer couldn't understand why my dad was making such a big deal out of picking 2 top runners and the conversation got a little heated. My dad doesn't remember exactly how the conversation went, but he does remember telling the writer that he could send a photographer, but he would not be taking a picture of just 2 runners. He could take a picture of the *team* and write the story about the *team*, and that was it.

My dad's decision was absolutely the right one. This group of young men worked together and each had an important part in the overall success of the team. Two runners could not win a meet or Invitational. It took the whole team, so my dad didn't back down. When the photographer arrived, the entire team of 7 was ready. And when the photographer questioned why 7 runners were present, he was told, "Sir, we are a team. It's all or nothing. End of discussion."

That day no pictures were taken for the paper; however, something more important than press coverage occurred. By standing his ground, my dad reinforced the fact that each of his runners was as valuable as the next, and consequently, each runner felt like #1. He consistently coached by the mantra, "You are what you think you are," and he dedicated his career to instilling that belief system into his athletes. But most, of all, *he* believed in each and every one of them, and with that kind of endorsement, they couldn't help but believe in themselves.

Sure, there were *stand out* players and runners over the years, and they did receive a lot of attention from the fans and the press, but my dad felt it was important to always have the Blue Mound Knights represented as a *team*. This philosophy kept the motivation high and kept each player or runner feeling like #1.

"Win...That's What They Do"

When you are number 1, everyone is gunning for you. There is a lot of pressure for top competitors, especially if they haven't been beaten all season. Back in the spring of 1979, Dick McDonald's mile relay team was gearing up for the State Track Meet, attending one last large Invitational in Charleston, Illinois. Todd Logue, Rick Brown, Doug Collier, and Mike Jackson had cruised through their season as an undefeated mile relay team and had arrived at the Charleston Invitational as *the* team to beat.

At this particular Invitational, coaches were not allowed on the track or in the field. They were banned to the stadium to watch the events just like any other fan, so just prior to the start of the race, Coach McDonald made his way to a seat in the stands with a bird's eye view of his team. In the moments before the event, McDonald realized he was positioned dangerously close to a very anxious group of spectators chatting about the much-anticipated chance to watch the undefeated Blue Mound team. McDonald, intrigued by their comments, fought off a grin because he realized they had no idea who he was. Not wanting to give away his identity at this point, he sat silently listening and waiting, like the others, for his team to take the track.

Ordinarily, McDonald was not a big risk taker. If something worked, he would not mess with it, but that day he decided to change his strategy. As mentioned earlier, sometimes being at the top means you have nowhere to go but down. While he was confident in his team's ability, he knew the competition at this meet would be fierce with larger schools and faster times. McDonald wanted to maximize his team's talent by using the element of surprise. He had no way of knowing, however, how entertaining this strategy would be in the end.

The usual order of runners for the mile relay include the second fastest runner in the lead-off position, the 3rd fastest runner in the 2nd leg of the race, and the slowest runner of the team in the 3rd leg, leaving the fastest runner to finish the race. The strategy, of course, is to get a decent start, not lose too much ground in the middle, and rely on the fastest runner to finish strong. McDonald, knowing all four of his runners extremely well, decided to shake up the order a bit in hopes of throwing off the competition.

In the mile relay, all of the runners are extremely fast, especially at a large Invitational like Charleston. McDonald's team had 2 of these extremely fast runners, 1 who was just a little bit faster, and 1 who was simply beyond compare. He knew their capacities and their limits, so he laid out his game plan to his runners:

"Pokey (Todd Logue), you are running first. Listen to me, you are not racing them, you are racing *my* clock. You need to run your leg in 58 seconds. Don't worry if they are ahead of you. You run *your* race…58 seconds will win it for us. Understand?"

"Yes, Coach"

"Brown, you're running next. You're might be behind in the pack, but you'll gain some ground. You run your leg of the race in about 57 seconds. That'll win it for us."

"Yes, Coach."

"Collier, you're third. They're gonna slow down, and you are gonna make up some lost-ground. Jack (Mike Jackson), you're gonna catch whoever might be in front of you, and we are gonna win this thing."

"Yes, Coach," was the unanimous response.

It was quite a gamble, but just maybe pure genius. Other coaches might have worried about their runners losing confidence or botching hand-offs, but McDonald knew he had the two fastest quarter-milers on the track that day and the overall fastest team. He was not worried, so he sat back and enjoyed the conversations going on around him in the stands.

The start gun sounded and they were off. Todd Logue, no slouch of a runner but probably more comfortably placed in the 3rd leg, was off to a good start. He held his own for quite a distance but eventually, slowly, blended into the middle of the pack. McDonald sat in the stands keeping one watchful eye on his runner and the other on his stopwatch. Logue was holding up his end of the deal. He was behind some of the others but running *his* race. The spectators near McDonald, however, were quick to criticize.

"Wow, that's a disappointment. I thought Blue Mound would have a better start," one man said, shaking his head.

"Yeah, disappointing," his friend agreed.

McDonald was both annoyed and amused by their comments. As Logue finished his leg, McDonald checked his stopwatch, and he had run one of his fastest times. After a flawless hand-off, Brown was off and running. Just as McDonald had hoped, he was gaining a little ground. If Brown could deliver a 57 second run as planned, McDonald knew they could win. Brown, a fiery competitor, was not used to being behind at the hand off, and he was motivated by the runners in front of him. He was running a fantastic race, but Blue Mound was still not in the lead as anticipated. Although he was making some progress, the men in the stands were still disappointed in what they thought would be a better showing from the Blue Mound team.

"Looks like the Blue Mound team can't cut it after all," one man said.

McDonald was intently fixated on his stopwatch, but he could hear the jeers of his neighbors. At this point he chose to remain silent, waiting for Brown to finish his leg, hoping he would be on his time. And sure enough he was. At this point it became increasingly difficult to keep from commenting on the status of the race, but McDonald hid a grin as Doug Collier received the baton. Collier, my dad was sure, would be the fastest runner in the third leg of the race. He would make up precious ground and put his team in winning position. Collier did not disappoint. It was like everyone else was moving in slow motion, and he was exploding at lightening speed. Time-wise, McDonald's stopwatch showed his team to be in contention to win, but it still seemed as if there was a long ways to go. Collier's performance, however, did not go unnoticed by the talkative fans.

"Geeze, that kid is flying," one of the men said with newfound excitement.

"Now that's more like it," the other chimed in.

Finally, McDonald could not contain himself anymore. "You guys like him?" he asked with a grin.

"Yeah!" they both agreed.

"Wait until you see the next guy. You're gonna *love* him!"

With that, McDonald sat back and relaxed a bit. His first two runners had delivered, and even though it looked as if they were losing, they were winning. McDonald looked down at Logue and Brown who were on the track anxiously awaiting confirmation of their success. McDonald signaled a "thumbs up." They had both run one of their personal best times, and my dad could not have been prouder. He then proceeded to watch Collier pass runner after runner before handing off to Jackson. Jackson, a state champion half-miler, would surely not disappoint. As he took off with baton in-hand McDonald addressed his companions one last time.

"This race is over, fellas."

"Yea, Blue Mound just didn't have the stuff," one of the negative fans added.

"No, I mean Blue Mound is gonna win it," said McDonald confidently.

"It looks to me like he's got a lot of race to run for that to happen," the fan snapped.

"Yep, and he's runnin' it," McDonald said with a grin.

And running it he was. Jackson was swiftly sailing past his final challengers. The doubters in the stands were in awe...speechless, as they watched Jackson not only take the lead but extend it considerably before closing the win.

As Jackson crossed the finish line, McDonald got up to go congratulate his championship team, but before he could get out of earshot, one of the men hollered, "How did you know they were going to win?"

McDonald slowly turned to address this ridiculous question, "Because I'm their coach," he proudly offered, "and that's what they do." With that said, McDonald turned and headed down the bleachers. The once talkative fans were dumbfounded. McDonald, grinning from ear to ear, was taking great satisfaction in the fact that this was the first time those guys had been quiet all day.

Coach's Note:

This win was an exceptional team effort. One cannot overlook the tremendous job Logue and Brown did. They actually had the toughest part of the race. It is hard to run your guts out when you are not in close contention with the other runners. I had such confidence in these guys. Collier and Jackson had the fun part of the race, catching and passing runners, which they both could do so well. Without the exceptional efforts of the first 2 runners, even outstanding runners like Collier and Jackson could not have caught the others.

Dennis Noland, a junior, was the regular member of this mile relay team, and Doug Collier usually ran the 440 yd. dash. This being the last race of the regular season, I wanted to run an all-senior team. Throughout the season, Dennis helped Blue Mound's mile relay team win the Arthur Invitational, the Pana Open, the Meridian Conference, the Macon County, and numerous other dual and triangular meets. Dennis was on the team that qualified for and ran in the State Track meet. I felt Dennis's name needed to be mentioned here because he was a valuable member of this mile relay team.

Coach

"My Girl Is Never Wrong"

Through his years as a coach, my dad always relied on a handful of others he could trust to collect valuable data concerning his players, runners, and teams. Especially during basketball games and track meets, my dad relied on his statisticians to keep meticulous records. In fact, if it wasn't for those records, much of the information in this book could not have been reported. My dad was a strategist, and he always critiqued the data collected from games and meets to plan for the future, so he had to get people he could trust to keep his stats. As far as he was concerned, there was no room for errors, so he hand-picked his statisticians every year, knowing the ones he chose could live up to his standards. One particular instance in the 1970's put one of my dad's statisticians to the test when he believed in her accuracy so much the Macon County Track Meet came to a screeching halt.

Terri Logue-Hill kept my dad's score book during track meets for the duration of her high school days. According to my dad she was the "chosen one" based on three factors: she had great communication skills; she was a perfectionist about *everything*; and finally, her math skills were beyond compare. So, in the 1970's when Blue Mound was beginning its run as a track powerhouse, Terri became a crucial part of my dad's team. I guess you could say, when every point counted, Coach McDonald wanted Terri to be the one counting them.

The Macon County Track Meet was and still is a rather large event with tough competitors. Somewhere around 1974, the Knights were a favorite to win, and Coach McDonald and his team were racking up points early in the meet. At large track meets there is always a scorers' box where the "official score keepers" keep track of the "official score" and then report it to the teams and spectators over a loud speaker. While my dad could not keep track of every point at all times, he always had some idea how his team was doing. At this particular time, he found himself a bit bewildered about the "official score." His mental calculations told him his team should be in first place, but that was not the verdict reported from the loud speaker.

Very soon after the puzzling announcement, Terri approached my dad, "Coach McDonald! They have the wrong score. We are ahead. Look," she said as she pointed to her score book, "see, we are ahead," she repeated with great urgency.

My dad trusted Terri unconditionally. Now, his gut-feeling about the score had been validated. If she said the official score was wrong, it was wrong. He quickly checked her numbers, grabbed the book, and headed for the scorers' box. He climbed the stairs to the small room perched far above the action, opened the door and announced, "Your score is wrong. I want this meet stopped until we get this straightened out."

Stopping a multi-school track meet indefinitely was a rather unorthodox event, but the gentlemen in the scorers' box took one look at my dad's face, and knew he meant business. Still, they were reluctant to cease all progress.

"Now, Coach, we keep the official score up here. I'm sure it's right," one of the men said, trying to appease my dad.

"No, it's not. I want this fixed now. I want this meet stopped until we get this mess fixed," my dad demanded.

"Ok, ok, Coach. How do you know, we are wrong?"

"I know because my girl has a different total. She says we are ahead," my dad insisted.

The men in the scores' box smiled. "Coach, we have the right score. Your girl is wrong," one replied.

"No, you don't understand," my dad snapped back. "My girl is not wrong. My girl is never wrong. You are going to check your numbers one by one next to hers, and we are not starting this meet again until you do." At that point the meet was officially put on hold.

"Ok, let's see her book," one said grudgingly. He took the book and began to compare the numbers. Several minutes later, he became fixated on one portion of the book where the numbers did not match. He recalculated them several times, and then finally looked up at my dad and said, "You're right. Your girl is right. We made a mistake." He quickly amended the error, announced the accurate score and the track meet continued.

Satisfied, my dad took Terri's book, descended the stairs and found Terri waiting for him at the bottom. She had a big smile on her face. When my dad came face to face with her, he said, "Thanks!"

"I told you they were wrong," she said.

"I didn't doubt you for a minute," he replied. "Now let's go win a track meet."

Terri Logue-Hill pictured here with a clipboard and Teresa Brown with a stopwatch, keep careful records at a track meet in 1975. This picture is from the 1975 yearbook.

"It's Not Whether You Win or Lose –
It's How You Play the Game"

It's true, the Blue Mound Knights had an awesome tradition of winning during the Coach McDonald Era, but I think many of his players, and Coach himself would agree that winning wasn't everything. My dad loved to win, but most of the time he was more concerned with the *effort* put forth by his players. Let's face it, no one can win all of the time. Concerning losing, my dad's philosophy was, "If you have to lose, you better play like a winner." Therefore, there were a few times when the Knights lost, but received no reprimands or harsh words. These were the nights when my dad's team fought hard, played to win, and never gave up; but in the end, they fell short of their goal. These losses were tolerated because there was effort and teamwork and a fiery competitive spirit alive in each player.

There is, however, another side of that scenario. Occasionally, the Knights posted a "W" in the books to find an irate coach who was critical and punishing. You see, a *win* didn't mean anything if it was half-hearted, sloppy, or effortless. Many, many times coaches and fans from other teams criticized my dad for running-up the score. It's true, the Blue Mound Knights, by nature, could not back-off when an opponent was sub par. Even when my dad would sub-in from the bench, these players played with the same tenacity as his starters. None of my dad's players were allowed to slack off as a courtesy. He coached and they played every game like it was the most important game in their lives. There were no easy wins. Likewise, he expected his players to play every game like it could be their last, and for the most part, they delivered.

One year -- I am not sure exactly when even though I have heard this story many times – the Knights were matched with a struggling team for their Homecoming game. Needless to say, their motivation and effort were not stacking up to my dad's standards. He grew increasingly frustrated through the first half, knowing many past players had returned for the Homecoming events. My dad worried that his former players would not be impressed with the quality of basketball they were seeing. So even though the

Knights held a considerable lead throughout the first half, my dad found himself as agitated as he would be if they were losing.

During the half-time break, my dad wasted no time chewing out his team, reprimanding them for sloppy errors and an overall lack of motivation. Amidst this tirade, the officials had made their way into my dad's office to relax during the break. That night one referee was a veteran who had worked many games for my dad. He entered the locker room office, grabbed a pop out of the fridge and commenced relaxing, somewhat oblivious to the racket my dad was making out in the locker room. The other referee was a young guy who hadn't had the experience of working a game for Blue Mound yet. He was completely bewildered by my dad's reaction at half time. He stood, confused, for many seconds and then spoke to his partner, "What's going on? Did I miss something?"

"What do you mean?" the veteran referee replied.

"What's he so pissed about?" The young referee asked, but then he didn't even wait for a reply. He headed out of the office and back up the stairs to check the score. The scoreboard confirmed what he had thought to be true. Blue Mound was winning by 21 points. Still confused, he headed back down to the locker room and back into my dad's office.

"Christ, he's winning by 21 points. Why is he so pissed?" the young referee said, as confused as ever.

"Yeah," his partner offered with a grin. "You outta hear him when they are losing."

The young referee just shook his head and grinned. That night he was introduced to Coach McDonald and Blue Mound basketball. From that moment on, he became one of those veteran referees who understood that the numbers on the scoreboard would not necessarily dictate the mood in the locker room. I'm sure every time he returned to work a game in Blue Mound, he remembered his first half-time experience with Coach McDonald.

This picture was released to Coach from the Decatur Herald and Review. It appears he is heading to the locker room, probably for a halftime "pep talk." Pictured from left to right: Bill Younger, Todd Logue, Rick Brown, Jim Brown, Mike Peer.

"Keep Your Eyes on the Ball"

Before a coach is a coach, he is usually an athlete. For many, the love for coaching is fueled by prior successes, knowledge of the game, and even by one's own shortcomings. All of this is true regarding my dad. Before he ever coached a game, he got lots of experience playing. One might think my dad was a basketball player, and he was. However, basketball was never the sport in which he excelled. Ironically, the sport my dad was most successful in as an athlete is also the sport he coached the least – baseball.

My dad only coached baseball for 4 years at Blue Mound High School. In those 4 years, however, he had a winning season every year and won the Meridian Conference in his final year, 1967. For anyone who knows my dad, you know that he took all his practices seriously. In baseball his practices usually had 3 parts: batting practice, situation plays, and simulated games. Serious as he may have been, my dad always tried to incorporate a little humor if appropriate, and this humor usually came in the form of some good old fashioned teasing.

One story I love to hear my dad tell involves a simulated game. In the simulated game practices the defensive players would take their positions with the pitcher on the mound and the catcher at the plate. My dad would use a fungo bat to hit the ball and runners would run the bases while the fielders would try to get them out. The fungo bat was the key to this drill because the ball would really jump off the bat, and if my dad put a little *heat* behind it, a pop fly could literally disappear into the clouds.

The object of the game was for the "home" team – the fielders – to deny the "visitors" any runs. My dad had a unique advantage in this game because he manipulated everything. He set the home team's score, he controlled where he hit the ball. He controlled how hard he hit the ball…he controlled everything. Likewise, my dad had a rule that if you made an error that cost Blue Mound the game, you had to run 2 times around the track. This rule applied to both practice games and real games. Obviously, players didn't want to be the one who made this error, but unfortunately, it sometimes happened, especially in the simulated games where my dad was calling all the shots.

Once in a practice game, my dad set the home team score as usual, and the fielders were doing their best to defend that score by not allowing any errors. My dad was really letting them have it by testing the infielders with challenging grounders and pop flies. He was also smashing them into the outfield and hitting line drives, hoping that even with these challenging tests, they could hold their own and win the game.

In this game there was a player on 2nd base named Bucky, and my dad loved to tease him. In an attempt to catch the home team off guard, my dad cranked a pop fly in Bucky's direction. It sailed up into the sky and Bucky called it, but he failed to get under it and missed the catch. Consequently, this error caused the visitors to score and ultimately win the game. With this outcome, Bucky had no choice but to hit the track and run his 2 laps.

While I am positive my dad did not want Bucky to make an error, the fact that he did set him up for a season full of good old fashioned teasing. Over the course of the season, every time the score was close and it looked like the home team was in trouble, my dad would fire a pop fly up into the sky right in Bucky's direction. He would hit the ball so hard it would zing up into the air and everyone would lose sight of it for several seconds. When it would reappear it would be heading in Bucky's direction, but Bucky would get so nervous he would miss the catch and a little grin would appear on my dad's face. He knew and everyone else knew that the fungo bat caused the ball to go faster and farther than any ball in a real game. My dad thought it was great fun to wait until the game was close and blast one up in Bucky's direction. After a few of these hilarious errors, Bucky knew he was being set up. The next time this happened, he was the one with the last laugh.

Once again, the simulated game score was close. There were 2 outs in the last inning and the bases were loaded, so the time was right to ding one up to Bucky at 2nd base. My dad tossed the ball up, reared back and gave it such a smack that it zipped into the sky at lightning speed. My dad had really outdone himself on this one. When Bucky looked up and saw the tiny ball above him still sailing upwards, he took off his glove and started jogging towards the track. When he got back the whole team was waiting and smiling. My dad asked him, "Bucky, why didn't you try to catch that ball?"

Bucky replied, "I looked up and that ball was so high it looked like an aspirin. I felt I could just save some time and head for the track."

To this reply my dad grinned and was not mad because he knew he had been targeting Bucky all year. Today, my dad and Bucky are great friends and this story comes up quite often when they get together to reminisce about the good old days.

Baseball was my dad's favorite sport to play from early grade school through high school. Ironically, it is the sport he coached the least during his career. My dad is pictured here ready to play at about age 12.

Note:

The previous stories in this section are my dad's stories that I have rewritten from my perspective; but when he gave me this one, I felt it was better said with his own voice.

"The Wife Speaks"

The only time my wife ever said anything to me about my coaching style was after a tough home game early in my career. Her words went something like this:

"Honey, I would like to share something with you. I think when you call a timeout, you should have the players come to you on the bench rather than meeting them halfway out on the court. They should come to you and sit on the bench so you can have your back to the fans. I got embarrassed tonight when everybody on our side of the floor could hear every word out of your mouth. I don't think the moms and dads should be able to hear your opinion about how their son is playing."

From that moment on, I took her advice and changed my timeout style. In 22 years of coaching and 51 years of marriage, I have learned… when the wife speaks, I listen.

Through a Daughter's Eyes

- "Reliving the Dream"

- "The Sweet Life of Being a Coach's Kid"

- "Summer Nights"

- "Subtle Wisdom"

- "Love and Basketball"

- "Here's to the Boys in Green

"Reliving the Dream"

If someone would have told me a year ago I would be helping my dad write a book about his coaching career, I would not have believed it. In fact, this book didn't start as a *book* at all. It began as a fact finding mission for my dad who wanted to nominate David Pistorius (Class of 1975) for the Illinois Basketball Hall of Fame.

Sometime in the fall of 2011, my dad began digging through his old score books, yearbooks, newspaper clippings, and personal notes to prepare a nomination packet for Pistorius. When he had all of his *ammunition*, so to speak, he asked me if I would type it for him. In the process of preparing the packet, I thought it would be the perfect time to help my dad organize *all* of his facts, statistics, and memoirs – something I have wanted to do for some time now. At first, when I mentioned it to him, he was reluctant and seemed disinterested, so I dropped it, but I did not completely dismiss the idea. Then one day in the winter of 2012 my dad asked about my ideas for the book. We began talking about it, and he became more receptive to the idea. Finally, after a little prodding from my mom, he agreed to help.

From that moment on, he spent countless hours at the Blue Mound Memorial Library scouring told yearbooks. He spent days, literally, digging through the boxes of newspaper clippings, photos, cards, and letters he had saved. When he would get a portion organized, he would give it to me to write up and type, and he would continue to research the details of his own life.

By late winter, my dad was notified that Pistorius would be inducted in the Basketball Players' Hall of Fame in April 2012. With this hurdle cleared, my dad began working on a Hall of Fame nomination packet for Gary Jackson (Class of 1977).

By the end of the summer, my dad had Jackson's nomination packet ready for the Hall of Fame Committee. He worried that a small town like Blue Mound would not get considered for 2 Hall of Fame players in the course of 2 years, but, ultimately, he felt the facts could speak for themselves. He left Jackson's packet with Bruce Firchau the day of his Illinois Basketball Hall of Fame

Museum interview. Sometime in the early months of 2013, we should find out if Jackson joins his high school and college teammate on the Hall of Fame wall.

With the completion of Jackson's nomination packet, it was time for my dad and I to get serious about finishing the book. The next chapter seemed to literally revolve around his Hall of Fame interview conducted in McDonald Gymnasium August 7, 2012. While this whole process had been an emotional rollercoaster for me, none of my experiences were as moving as watching my dad relive some of the best times of his life during that interview.

My dad was both nervous and excited about this interview, and he had reminded me of it many times over the course of the summer. Initially, I just wanted to snap a few pictures for the book, but that day and that experience grew into much more for me. I literally got chills when I pulled up to the school and again when I entered the gymnasium lobby. This was the lobby where I sat and did homework as a grade school student waiting for my dad's practices to end. This was the lobby where I practiced cheers with my teammates, and the same lobby I entered for every Blue Mound Knights home game I cheered at or watched. I know it seems crazy, but I was completely caught off guard by the powerful feelings this place created.

If that wasn't enough, going into the actual gym was even more overwhelming. I remembered it as mostly blue and white, but now it is entirely green, except for the sign that announces it as McDonald Gymnasium. I got chills when I stood on the sidelines where I cheered for 4 years. It was all incredibly nostalgic.

For the interview my dad and Bruce sat in folding chairs at center court. They talked about my dad's humble beginnings at Boody Grade School, and they spoke of Bob Miller who was the varsity basketball coach at Blue Mound when my dad was hired as an assistant in 1964. They spoke of rival teams and coaches and exceptional players. They talked about my dad's coaching philosophy, the image and behavior of his players, the secrets of his offense and defense, and, of course, they spoke of the exceptional shooting for which his teams became known. All the while, I sat, mesmerized, by the conversation as if it was the first time I had ever heard these stories. I was captivated by the ease with which my dad recalled names and dates and events, as if it had occurred just yesterday instead of decades ago. And that's when it hit me…even though I had known it all along, it hit me. Coaching and these stories and that gym and all of his players truly were his *life*. He's older now and decades removed from coaching his last game, but he is still the same person who sat on the bench and orchestrated all of those well-executed ballgames. And with all of that responsibility to the school, the players and the fans, he was still a teacher, a husband, a father, and a son.

In his interview, my dad was asked about his marriage because being a coach's wife is not easy. He proudly responded that my mother's support was steadfast from their beginnings back at Boody. He said she never complained about the long hours and the time away from home because she knew he was happy. Then, almost shyly, he thanked her for her unwavering support throughout his career, and he seemed to almost apologize for his time away from home throughout those years. He also thanked his parents for their support and encouragement throughout his career. He thanked my grandpa, who despite a 60 mile commute, held a season ticket and never missed a home game. He spoke of my grandma who was very crippled with arthritis and unfortunately could not attend games, but he appreciated the fact that she never missed one that was broadcast on the radio. And as he spoke of these special people in his life, I was overcome with emotion, never realizing that he relied so heavily on the love and support of family.

It was truly a memorable day, and at some point I felt like a kid again, and I bet my dad also felt like that robust, competitive coach who sat the bench and walked the sideline for 22 years. I just want to thank my dad for that day and for allowing me to relive that very special time in our lives. For anyone who played, cheered, kept stats or watched from the stands during my dad's coaching days, I can tell you he considers you all friends who contributed to the best times of his life.

"The Sweet Life of Being a Coach's Kid"

Growing up a coach's kid was really rather ordinary, but I have a few favorite memories that stand out. Even after all this time, I remember some of these events as if they were yesterday. I loved growing up as Coach McDonald's daughter, and I still love it today.

One of the fondest memories I have from my grade school days is attending basketball parties after Friday night ballgames. After the first home game every season, my parents would have a party with all of their "teacher friends." That night each of the friends would sign up for a Friday night game and host a party. That meant my brother and I would spend every Friday night watching *Tales of Terror* with Cheryl and Eddie Morr and Paula Cawthon. We would eat and drink pop and entertain ourselves any way we could without drawing the attention of the adults. Those were good times, and I know my dad thinks so, too.

Also from my grade school days are my memories of walking to the high school after school and entering my dad's world of basketball practice. From about 1st grade to about 5th grade in the cold basketball months, I would walk from the grade school to the high school when the school day was finished. I didn't go home because my mom was still at work and would not be home until after 5pm. Sometimes before my dad's basketball practice began, he would give me .25 for a bottle of pop. There was an old pop bottle machine in the lobby and the soda that came out of there was the coldest, best soda in the world, or at least I remember it that way. So for a few hours I would explore the world of the high school halls, the stage, locker rooms and even the secluded space behind the bleachers while my dad was conducting basketball practice. I was pretty much allowed to come and go as I pleased, as long as I didn't make noise. Most of the time, my dad never even knew I was there. A few times, however, when I was playing behind the bleachers, he called out for me and told me to go out in the lobby. At those times, I knew to hurry out because something bad was probably going to happen. But those times were few and far between. Most of the time, I was in my own little world running the halls and playing make-believe. After practice was over, the players would sometimes joke around with me, and I was on top of the world. These are fond, fond memories of my dad and my childhood.

In the fall of every school year before the weather got too cold, I would spend much of my after-school time riding my bike. This was the time of year my dad was practicing cross country and the high school boys would be running a practice course around town. My friend LeAnn and I would get great pleasure watching these boys take off on their 3 mile trek with my dad cruising behind them in his Blazer 4x4. And when I say "cruising" I mean literally. He had a minimum cruising speed, and runners had to stay in front of his vehicle. I really don't know if everyone always kept his pace or if occasionally someone had to drop to the side, but he was quite the sight to see putt-putting down the road, chomping on his cigar with a pack of runners ahead of him. I imagine if you were the ones right in front of the truck, this activity would be rather nerve wracking, but it was a standard practice drill, and apparently, it was effective!

In the spring, just as in the fall and winter, I would make the trek from the grade school to the high school to be with my dad until my mom got home from work. Spring time was track season, and I would go outside and watch practice and enjoy the outdoors. When I was in about fourth grade, I decided to get a perm. I had short hair and a tight frizzy perm, which sounds absolutely awful, but for some reason it was the style then. The first day I showed up at track practice with my perm, a bunch of the high school boys started calling my Larry. I didn't know why, but I knew it had something to do with my hair. When I asked them, they said I looked like this boy in school who had a massive head of frizzy hair, and his name was Larry. Even though I knew they were kidding, I didn't care much for the nickname. Eventually my distaste for the name faded, and I just accepted that I was "Larry."

Every day for the better part of 4 years, my dad's runners and players would holler "Hi Larry!" every time they saw me. I'm not going to lie, at some point I began loving the attention. The only time I can remember NOT loving the attention was when I was doing the long jump at a junior high track meet and one of the high school boys yelled, "Go Larry!", and I ended up scratching on that pass. In the big scheme of things, that was a small price to pay for receiving years of attention from older high school boys. Yeah, looking back, being Larry was not so bad after all!

When I got in high school, I got to see my dad at school every day, and as awesome as it was when I needed lunch money or needed a permission slip signed, it was awkward and embarrassing when it came to dating. Despite his watchful eye, I did manage to have a social life. Over the years I dated a Comet, a Trojan, an Ironman, and, of course, a Knight. One might think my dad would frown on me seeing anyone but a Knight, but quite the contrary. In fact, he preferred it when I was dating the "enemy." I have to give all of those boys credit because it probably wasn't easy walking up those steps to my house for the first time, but they did it. And I think in the end they found out my dad is really just an ordinary guy.

My final memory is probably one of my favorites. My sophomore year, my dad bought an old truck we affectionately named "Old Blue." This truck was 3 different shades of blue, having a variety of replaced body-parts over the years. It had a pull choke and a gear shift on the column, two things I had never even seen before. The most notable feature, however, was a huge hole all the way though the floorboard on the passenger's side. I can remember being both intrigued and frightened watching the movement of the pavement as we were putt-putting down the road. For some reason my dad loved this truck, and he insisted on driving it to home ballgames or to catch the bus to away games. Being a cheerleader, I always rode with him, and quite often found myself a little embarrassed pulling up to the school with my dad in that old clunker.

Probably the worst time to ride in Old Blue was in the winter when there was snow on the ground. Even in the short distance from our house to the school, my feet and legs would be covered in snow. My senior year we had blue knee socks as part of our cheerleading uniform and that winter we also had a lot of snow. I would arrive at school with so much snow on my socks they looked completely white and stayed wet for most of the night. At the time it was very irritating, but now I see those trips to games with my dad in old blue as precious memories. I can still see my dad sitting in the driver's seat working the choke and the clutch and the gear shift, laughing all the way to the school.

The times I spent with my dad after school and in high school are some of my fondest memories. While most of these memories occurred decades ago, I remember them like they were just yesterday.

Old Blue outside my parents' home about 1984.

"Summer Nights"

In the summer of 1974, I was 8 years old. My days were spent riding my bike and swimming with friends at the local swimming pool. My evenings and nights were spent in my garage playing my Jackson 5 vinyl records and twirling my baton or making up dances. The garage was my sanctuary. No one bothered me. It was *my* place. Well, it *was* my place until one particular evening when my dad decided it was the perfect place to stand and watch the activity across the street at the park basketball courts.

For most of my early childhood, we lived across from the town park, and on summer nights the basketball court was hopping with activity. It might seem a little too convenient that the varsity basketball coach had a clear view of the local courts from his garage, but honestly, until that summer, my dad had little interest in what went on over there. He knew who was there every night and who wasn't. He didn't need to *watch* because he knew who had talent and who had their heart in the game. But that one summer night, he caught his first glimpse of a new player on the court, and suddenly I had company in the garage.

I was just out in the garage doing my thing, happy as can be, and my dad came out and stood right in the middle of the floor. For a minute I was really perplexed. He assumed the classic stance: feet at hips' width and arms folded. He didn't say a word. He stood silently staring straight forward. Finally, I figured out he was watching the boys in the park play basketball.

His presence made my dancing and twirling impossible, so I was extremely annoyed. At first, I refused to relinquish my sanctuary, and I mistakenly thought I could wait him out. But since I was just a little afraid to talk, and I didn't dare play my records, I gave up after about 10 minutes, when it was clear he was not leaving. The next night, it was the same thing. He stayed out there for hours, and I finally had to ask my mom why my sacred space was being invaded. I remember her saying, "There's this new basketball player who has moved to town. Your dad is checking him out."

That new player was sophomore Gary Jackson who had moved in from Niantic-Harristown High School. Looking back, I can see exactly why Gary caused such a stir. He ended up being the all-time leading scorer for the Blue Mound Knights. Today Gary and my dad are great friends who have mutual respect for one another. Back then, he was a young sharp-shooter who had hand-picked my dad as his coach and the Knights as his team. My dad was more than intrigued by what he saw at the park, and to my dismay, he did a lot of watching that summer. When school started in the fall, he knew more about Gary and his talent than even Gary knew.

In the end, losing my special place was not so bad. I moved the record player in the house and commenced creating. That summer my dad could not have known for sure that Gary Jackson would help lead the Blue Mound Knights to 7 championships and 69 wins during his sophomore, junior and senior years, but I imagine he was fairly certain something amazing was on the horizon. And so he watched, silently, and smiled.

"Subtle Wisdom"

Growing up, I sometimes felt like I was part of a team instead of part of a family. I guess when your dad is busy coaching 3 sports, every season is an *in season*, even for family. Don't get me wrong; I'm not complaining. I think I turned out pretty good, comparatively. Looking back, I see that my dad's parenting style was much like his coaching style. He mostly used an approach that was motivational. He had, and still has, this way of getting a person to uncover his inner-best. Today I have come to know this "game plan" – for the lack of a better term – as *subtle wisdom*. You see, he has this way of cleverly mentioning something that makes a person think, and the more that person thinks about it, the more it positively influences him. Putting this tactic into words is extremely difficult, but I am fairly certain anyone who ever played on one of my dad's teams knows exactly what I'm talking about. It's one of those weird contradictions…something so simple, it's complicated.

I have pretty much grown to be the person I am today based on many pieces of this subtle wisdom. Growing up I would hear these sayings frequently, and at times dismiss them, but this dismissal was only temporary. My dad's words, and more importantly the *meaning* of those words, still resonate in my head today. I honestly feel the entire core of my belief system links directly back to two specific examples of his subtle wisdom.

It never failed. I would be getting ready to go out with friends or go out on a date and before I could zip out the door my dad would offer these words of advice: "Marceleda, don't out-drive your headlights!" This famous metaphor was meant to detour just about anything that could end up getting me in trouble. Over the years it meant all of the following and more:

> Don't do something you will regret later.
> Don't do something for the wrong reasons.
> Don't get yourself into something you cannot get out of.
> Don't do something just because everyone else is doing it.
> Don't think you are invincible.

Don't think you can't get caught.

Don't get wrapped up in something you cannot handle.

Well, you get the picture. So every time I even *thought* about doing something even a *little* questionable, I heard his words resonating inside my head. I am a lot like my dad: practical, cautious, and self-respecting. I thought too much of my dad, and myself, to risk disappointing either. "Don't out drive your headlights," still has real meaning for me. And occasionally when my dad thinks I need a little reality check, he will remind me, the way a dad should: "Marceleda, don't out drive your headlights."

While that saying kept me grounded and honest, the next one instilled self confidence and pride. Growing up, I was always proud to be Marcy McDonald. I was raised to have goals and to not make excuses for my shortcomings. I didn't have to be perfect at anything, but I had to be my best. Part of this attitude originates from my dad's other favorite saying: "Marceleda, you are who you think you are!" As long as I believed in myself, I could do anything. If *I* thought I was a winner, then I was winner. This saying taught me that my destiny was within my control. I may not be able to control anyone else or anything else, but I was in control of *me*. More specifically, I was a McDonald and that meant something to my dad, and he felt it should mean something to me…and it does. Still today, when I feel challenged or maybe even a little overwhelmed and defeated, I think of these words: "You are who you think you are." And if I sit around and feel sorry for myself, then I'm pathetic and miserable and that's my choice. But if I want more for myself, I have to make it happen. I feel so blessed to have had such subtle wisdom come my way. I think a lot of my dad's former athletes and students probably feel the same.

Sure, my dad could be direct and thunderously clear when it came to getting his point across, but he also knew when subtlety was the best approach. His subtle messages of "Don't out drive your headlights" and "You are who you think you are" were not confrontational, preachy, or authoritative. They were, as I have said before, pieces of subtle wisdom, cleverly offered at the opportune time for effectiveness. His approach was genius, and I will say I have not hesitated using this approach with my own girls. After all, my dad always said, "If you are winning, why change horses in the middle of the race?" I'll let you ponder that bit of subtle wisdom, compliments of my dad.

"Love and Basketball"

Every little girl dreams of her wedding day and walking down the aisle with her father. I was no exception. But when you plan a wedding for the end of February and your dad is a high school basketball coach, there's going to be some tension.

Most people don't arrange their lives around high school basketball, but my family is a little different. For my entire childhood and part of my adulthood, it was as if the rest of the world stopped November 1 through the first of March to allow high school basketball to run its course for another year. As I grew older and left my parents' home, I forgot the vacuum of "all things basketball" still controlled their every move. Unfortunately, back in 1990, the plan God had for me was in direct conflict with the IHSA Boys' Basketball schedule.

In November of 1989, I found out I was pregnant. Upon hearing this news, my fiancé and I considered two factors when setting the wedding date. First of all, I wanted to wear a wedding dress and not look pregnant even though most people knew I was. The second factor was very practical and was directly linked to the availability of the Knights of Columbus Hall. At the time, my fiancé was a member, and we were going to be able to save a significant amount of money by having the reception there. After these two factors were considered, the date we chose was February 23rd.

I'll never forget the look on my dad's face when we told him. Now, keep in mind, we set the date in December, yet the first words out of his mouth were, "That's the Regional final." I think my response was, "So?" The rest of the conversation played out something like this:

"You can't get married on the night of the Regional final."

"Why not?"

"Because I won't be there."

At this point I think my mom chimed in, which was rare but always necessary, "Dick, what do you mean you won't be there?"

"We're going to be playing."

He said it just like that, very matter-of-factly. I didn't know whether to laugh or cry. Looking back now, I see his words as no big surprise. I had grown up in a house where basketball was *king,* and although my dad was a great dad and was always there for me when I needed him, he had another love – basketball. I knew right then I had messed up because, if, in fact, the Blue Mound Knights were scheduled to play in the Regional final, my dad would have a VERY difficult decision to make. Needless to say, I was disappointed. I was disappointed in myself for not realizing this conflict existed, and I was disappointed in him for even considering choosing basketball over me.

I could tell my dad was disappointed, too. After all these years of living through season after season, he thought I should know the routine. At one point he pretty much asked us if we could change the date. We couldn't. So we went day by day through the 1990 season walking on eggshells, not knowing how the end would play out. While I wanted my dad to be successful that season, I also wanted him to be at my wedding and be there of his own free will, not wishing he was somewhere else. To my dismay, the Knights were having a winning streak in the latter part of their season, and as my wedding day approached, I feared the worst.

In the end, my dad was at my wedding and walked me down the aisle because the Knights didn't make it to the final game. I have often thought, however, about how things might have played out in the alternative scenario. As a daughter of a basketball coach - a winning basketball coach - you don't want to think your dad would choose a game over you. But it was not just a *game*; it was his way of life, and this game affected more than just him and me. We are talking about players and their families and a whole town, really. What kind of coach would abandon his team in a Regional final game? On the flip-side, what kind of dad would not walk his daughter down the aisle so he could coach a basketball game?

Thankfully, we will never know.

Father – Daughter Dance
February 23, 1990

I posted a similar version of the following article on Facebook in March 2009 just after the Meridian Hawks boys' basketball team advanced to State play. It received numerous comments from former Blue Mound Knights who are raising their children as Meridian Hawks. It just goes to show that Blue Mound is still a "basketball town." I prefer to think that my dad had just little bit to do with that.

"Here's to the Boys in Green!"

I guess you could say being a basketball fan is in my blood. When you grow up in Blue Mound and have the name *McDonald* you don't really have a choice. As a very young child I remember going to games and watching the cheerleaders and even being a mascot one year with Diane Noland, Linda Younker, and lots of others who are captured in a black and white photo on display in my parents' trophy case. The year was about 1971.

In the late seventies, I was in junior high and still watched the cheerleaders, but I also became fascinated with the actual game. It became habit to begin to clap or cheer *before* the basketball actually went through the hoop when Gary Jackson shot or Brad Eckols put it up from the corner. It didn't matter which corner; he wasn't picky that way. Today's players are rewarded with 3 points for those shots. I often wonder what the 3-point advantage would have done for my dad's teams of the 70's, and I know my dad wonders too.

In the mid-eighties, I was in high school and once again Blue Mound had an awesome team. It was the same team Coach Larry Rosenthal took to state as 8th graders. In 1984, as seniors, this team was only beaten once in regular season play. Can you guess by whom?? Yes, the Macon Ironmen. It was late in the season at Blue Mound, a neck and neck nail-biting dual to the finish. In the end, a Knight (who shall remain nameless), missed a free throw - something that rarely happened - and the Ironmen won. The Knights weren't beaten again until post-season play in the Sectional. Which finally brings me to my point: This year people from these two towns are enjoying the fruits of decades of tradition and pride, and I say, "It's about time!"

In my dad's day, the Illinois basketball system did not differentiate between large schools and small schools the same way it does now. It sounds crazy, but my dad recalls playing against Springfield Lanphier in a Regional final back in the 70's. The Knights lost, but played as a respectable adversary. Today, it is so much better not to have to compare apples to oranges, so to speak. Small schools have the awesome opportunity to showcase their talent and compete in state play on a reasonable level. Again, I say, "It's about time!"

I often wonder, and I'm sure my dad does too, if any of his teams could have made it to state if the 4 class system was in effect then. But then I think…it doesn't really matter. Good basketball is still good basketball, and I've seen the Hawks play enough this year to know …THEY PLAY GOOD BASKETBALL. My dad knows, too. He can't go to games. He can't be just a *spectator*. But his absence is not because he is indifferent to it all. He knows...oh boy, does he know...and he takes it all in with a grin. He's more than a little sad that McDonald Gymnasium no longer hosts high school games and that on Friday nights the lights off, but it's just a few miles down the road where the tradition continues. This is a year tradition turns to history, and this former Knight has no problem cheering for the boys in green.

Statistics and Highlights:
4 Sports
4 Decades

- Boody Grade School
- Baseball
- Basketball
- Track
- Cross Country

Boody Grade School

BULLETS

1961 – 1962
1962 - 1963

Boody Grade School 1961

Boody Grade School
BULLETS

After graduating from Illinois State University in the spring of 1961, Mr. McDonald was hired by the Blue Mound School District to teach junior high science for the 1961 – 62 school year at Boody Grade School. Boody is a small, rural town that was part of the Blue Mound school district but had its own grade school up until the mid-1970's. At the time Mr. McDonald was hired, he was assigned coaching duties for 2 sports: basketball and baseball. That first year Coach McDonald coached 5th and 6th grade basketball; 5th, 6th, 7th, 8th grade baseball; and served as the assistant coach for the 7th and 8th grade basketball teams.

The following school year (1962 – 63), Coach McDonald was reassigned to coach baseball and 5th and 6th grade basketball but was also asked to coach 7th and 8th grade basketball. In addition, he began coaching the $5^{th} – 8^{th}$ grade boys track teams.

In those 2 years at Boody Grade School, Coach McDonald was completing a Masters degree in Psychology at Illinois State University. This addition to his credentials secured his job as high school guidance counselor and biology teacher with coaching duties at Blue Mound High School for the 1963-64 school year.

BOODY GRADE SCHOOL COACHING

1962	Baseball	5th, 6th, 7th, 8th
	Basketball	5th, 6th
	Basketball Asst.	7th, 8th
1963	Baseball	5th, 6th, 7th, 8th,
	Basketball	5th, 6th, 7th, 8th
	Track	5th, 6th, 7th, 8th

*There are no records available for this portion of Coach McDonald's career.

Coach's Tidbit

Coach McDonald had 3 players who played for him in 6th and 7th grade at Boody and then again all 4 years at Blue Mound High School. These 3 were 6th graders McDonald's first year at Boody Grade School (1961-62) and graduated from Blue Mound High School in 1968.

Ken Huffman
HS Baseball 4 years
HS Track 1 year
HS Basketball 4 years

Kirk Sunderland
Track 1 year
Basketball 4 year

John Pistorius
Baseball 4 years
Basketball 4 years

1st Baseball Team
Boody Grade School Bullets 1961-62
1st Row (kneeling): John Ferguson, Bill Augustine, Mike Damery, Jim Weybright, Ken Huffman
2nd Row (standing): Paul Etherton, Gay Helm, Ken Etherton, John Brown, Chuck Plunkett, Don Ferguson, Rick Pinnell, John Pistorius, Kirk Sunderland, Gary Armstrong.
Coach McDonald standing in back.

First 5th & 6th Grade Basketball Team
Boody Grade School Bullets 1961-62

1st Row (sitting): Mike Damery, Rick Pinnell, John Brown, Bill Augustine, Ken Huffman 2nd Row (standing): Jim Getz, Charles McGorray, Tom Logsdon, Paul Etherton, Paul Jenkins, Ross Nelson, Jim Weybright, Gary Jacobs, Coach McDonald

McDonald's first 7th and 8th Grade Team
Boody Grade School 1962-63.

L to R: Ken Huffman, John Ferguson, Bill Augustine, Gene Dietz, Don Ferguson, John Pistorius

Boody Grade School Cheerleaders 1962-63:
Bev Pistorius, Diana Damery, Sheila Oxford, Patti Hadden, Jane Huffman

Blue Mound
High School

KNIGHTS

1964 – 1991

This picture of Blue Mound High School was taken from the 1973 yearbook.

The Blue Mound Knights &
Coach McDonald
A Winning Combination

When people think of Coach McDonald and his history with the Blue Mound Knights, they probably mostly remember his remarkable basketball career. What some people may not realize is McDonald's coaching success was not isolated to one sport. For most of McDonald's career, he coached in every season and attained the same level of success as he achieved coaching basketball. Something else people may not realize is that for most of Coach McDonald's career, the IHSA did not divide schools into 1A, 2A, 3A, and 4A the way they do today. In McDonald's day, it was not uncommon for Blue Mound, a high school of around 175 students, to be matched against schools three times its size, or more.

Coach McDonald's winning tradition at Blue Mound High School began in the 1963-64 school year when he became the varsity baseball coach and the junior varsity basketball coach. Incidentally, that year his junior varsity basketball team earned an 18 – 0 record. From this humble beginning, a remarkable coaching career developed. This career would go on to span 4 decades, suffer 2 resignations, and embrace 2 comebacks, not to mention generate an outpouring of school spirit, a tradition of success, and an impressive sports history that ultimately amassed 87 multi-school championships in 49 seasons. The facts, statistics, and stories chronicled here attempt to honor a remarkable coaching career that has secured Coach McDonald's place in Central Illinois sports history.

BASEBALL

One of Dick McDonald's first varsity coaching assignments was Boys' Baseball. In his four years as coach, McDonald chalked up a winning season all 4 years and won 40 of 56 total games and 1 championship. Despite an impressive record, after the 1967 season, McDonald retired from coaching baseball to concentrate on coaching basketball and running sports.

YEAR	WINS	LOSSES	CHAMPIONSHIPS
1964	7	3	
1965	7	2	
1966	12	4	
1967	14	7	Meridian Conference

Coach McDonald's First Varsity Baseball Team (1964)
Picture from the 1964 yearbook.

STANDING: McDonald, Sperry, Albers, Snyder, Naber, Logue, P. Brown, Cripe
KNEELING: Hill, Wellwood, Reed, J. Brown, Pistorius, Weybright, Zeeb
SITTING: Boggs, Nolen, Davis, McVey, Hutton, Gorden, Buckner, K. Brown

Varsity Baseball

1964 Team
* Denotes Varsity Letter Winner

*Ron Naber	Co-Captain	Phil Brown
*Larry Boggs	Co-Captain	Leon Wellwood
*Paul Sperry		Gary Weybright
*John Hill		Leon Zeeb
*Bob Albers		Ed Nolen
*Jay Brown		Mark Davis
*Alan Snyder		John McVey
*Jerry Logue		Kent Gorden
*Dan Hutton		Don Buckner
*Gayle Reed		Kim Brown
*Gene Pistorius		
*John McCoy		
Richard Cripe, Manager		

1965 Team
* Denotes Varsity Letter Winner

*Don Naber	Bill Augustine
*Paul Sperry	Ken Huffman
*Jay Brown	John Pistorius
*Pete Bankson	Jeff Nelson
*Kim Brown	*Gene Pistorius
*Dan Hutton	*Jerry Logue
*John McVey	*Kent Gorden
*Mark Davis	*Sam Pate
David Holtfreter, Manager	
Dan Sexson, Scorer	

1966 Team
* Denotes Varsity Letter Winner

*Dan Hutton	Pete Bankson
*John McVey	Gary Beck

*Jay Brown, Co-Captain
*Paul Sperry, Co-Captain
*Kim Brown
*Sam Pate
*Bill Clark
*Kent Gorden
*Ken Huffman
*John Pistorius
*Guy O'Bryan
David Holtfreter, Manager

Mike Scales
Leon Pruett
Mike Damery
Mike Maulding
Dean Sefried
Bill Augustine
Joe Zeeb

1967 Team
Meridian Conference Champions
14 W - 7 L
* Denotes Varsity Letter Winners

*Joe Zeeb
*Ken Huffman
*Pete Bankson
*Kim Brown
*Kent Gorden
*Sam Pate
*Guy O'Bryan
*Bob Barnfield
*John Pistorius
Bill Meyers, Assistant Coach

Leon Pruett
Donald Beck
Mike Maulding
Rob Buzan
Calvin Elder
Bill Huffman
*Gary Beck
*Dan Robinson
*Trent Wilcox

This photo appeared in
the *Decatur Herald and Review*
in the spring of 1966

Pictured here are teammates, co-captains, and friends, Jay Brown and Paul Sperry in 1966. Brown caught behind the plate as Sperry fired in the pitches from 5th grade all through high school. Sperry went on to pitch at Illinois State University where he earned a spot in the ISU Baseball Players' Hall of Fame. Sperry also signed a contract with the New York Giants minor league team.

BASKETBALL

Even though nearly 22 years have passed since Dick McDonald coached his last varsity basketball game, he is still known as *Coach*. His basketball coaching career at Blue Mound began in 1964 and lasted until his coaching retirement in 1991. Coach McDonald had retired twice before, the first time after the 1971 season. This break from the action, however, did not last long. McDonald did not coach the 1972 season but was back at the helm in 1973. Then after a health scare in 1984, McDonald stepped down again for the 1985, '86, and '87 seasons. Ultimately, he found it too hard to walk the halls of Blue Mound High School as a counselor and teacher and not also be a coach. So once again, he came out of retirement in 1988 to be the varsity basketball coach for the Blue Mound Knights.

During his extensive career, Coach McDonald compiled some impressive statistics. In his 22 year career, he led the Knights to 373 wins and endured only 193 losses. These statistics rank 172nd on the IHSA "Win List" published February 22, 2010. With McDonald at the helm, the Knights won 26 championships overall. From 1976 through 1979 McDonald and the Knights posted 42 consecutive wins in Meridian Conference games. Additionally, from 1970 through 1979 Blue Mound's Meridian Conference game record was an impressive 99 wins and 11 loses.

McDonald's achievements did not go unnoticed. He was named the Illinois Basketball Coaches' Association District "Coach of the Year" in 1979. In that same year he was named *The Decatur Herald and Review* Area "Coach of the Year." McDonald also has over 15 other plaques of honor and appreciation from the Blue Mound School Board, Millikin University, various teams, and the IBCA Hall of Fame. At the final home game February 19th, 1993, the gymnasium where he had built his legacy was named McDonald Gymnasium in his honor. Past players, cheerleaders, statisticians, score keepers, and other "friends of basketball" were in attendance on this momentous occasion. Then, on April 24th, 1993, Dick "Coach" McDonald was inducted into the Illinois Basketball Coaches Association Hall of Fame.

In August of 2012 he was interviewed by David Firchau for the Illinois Basketball Coaches Hall of Fame Museum in Danville. Firchau, a fellow coach and a member of the Board of Directors for the museum, met Coach McDonald at Meridian Middle School (formerly Blue Mound High School) and conducted the 50 minute interview in McDonald Gymnasium. Today, sports enthusiasts and basketball fans can tour the museum and watch the video interview which attempts to honor not only McDonald's accomplishments but also recognize past players, rival teams, and opposing coaches from McDonald's era.

Basketball Statistics

Year	Wins	Losses	Championships
1964 (JV)	18	0	
1965 (JV)	12	6	
1966 (JV)	15	3	
totals	45	9	
1966 (V)	21	8	District Tournament
1967 (V)	14	9	Meridian Conference
1968 (V)	15	10	
1969 (V)	18	8	
1970 (V)	23	4	Macon County Tournament
			Meridian Tournament
			Meridian Conference
			Regional Tournament
1971 (V)	16	7	Meridian Tournament
1972 (V)			DID NOT COACH

1973 (V)	12	12	
1974 (V)	21	6	Macon County Tournament
			Meridian Conference
			Regional Tournament
1975 (V)	24	2	Macon County Tournament
			Meridian Tournament
			Regional Tournament
1976 (V)	18	8	
1977(V)	27	1	Macon County Tournament
			Meridian Tournament
			Meridian Conference
			Regional Tournament
1978 (V)	26	1	Macon County Tournament
			Meridian Conference
			Meridian Tournament
			Regional Tournament
1979(V)	19	7	Meridian Conference
1980 (V)	19	7	
1981 (V)	5	18	
1982 (V)	8	17	
1983 (V)	20	9	Regional Tournament
1984 (V)	26	2	Meridian Conference
			Meridian Tournament
			Regional Tournament

1985 (V)			DID NOT COACH
1986 (V)			DID NOT COACH
1987 (V)			DID NOT COACH
1988 (V)	8	16	
1989 (V)	16	11	
1990 (V)	13	12	
1991 (V)	4	18	
1992			RETIRED FROM COACHING

Basketball Championship Totals

Macon County Tournament	Meridian Conference	Meridian Conf. Tournament	IHSA Regional Tournament	District Tournament
1970	1967	1970	1970	1966
1974	1970	1971	1974	
1975	1974	1975	1975	
1977	1977	1977	1977	
1978	1978	1978	1978	
	1979	1984	1983	
	1984		1984	

Meridian Conference Highlights

In 1995 Blue Mound High School combined with Macon High School to form the Meridian School District. The name, obviously, came from the former Conference compiled of 12 schools. Before consolidation, Coach McDonald and the Blue Mound Knights were considered a Powerhouse of the conference. In his 22 years of coaching from 1966 thru 1991, McDonald compiled 177 conference wins and only 65 losses.

In the decade of the 1970's, McDonald and the Knights posted 99 wins against their 11 conference opponents. Additionally, in that same decade, the Knights went on a 42 game winning streak in conference play. This streak lasted from the 1976 season through the end of the 1979 season.

True Champions

In his 22 years as Head Basketball Coach of the Blue Mound Knights, McDonald won a total of 26 championships. He and the Knights claimed the title of Macon County Tournament Champions 5 times in his career. He also won 6 Meridian

Conference Tournaments and 1 District Tournament. McDonald and the Knights were the Meridian Conference Champs 7 times during his reign, as well as IHSA Regional Champions an impressive 7 times.

Meridian Conference Game Statistics

Once a strong, solid conference, The Meridian Conference was dissolved in the late 1990's. Consolidations and school closings eventually forced schools to move elsewhere. During Coach McDonald's era, the Meridian Conference was made up of the 12 schools listed below.

1) Assumption Comets
2) Bethany Mustangs
3) Blue Mound Knights
4) Findlay Falcons
5) Illiopolis Pirates
6) Lovington Panthers
7) Macon Ironmen
8) Maroa-Forsyth Trojans
9) Moweaqua Indians
10) Niantic-Harristown Indians
11) Stonington Wildcats
12) Tower Hill Tigers

Blue Mound Knights' Conference Statistics

Year	Wins	Losses
1966	8	3
1967	9	2
1968	9	2
1969	9	2
1970	10	1
1971	9	2
1972	N/A	N/A

1973	9	2
1974	10	1
1975	10	1
1976	9	2
1977	11	0
1978	11	0
1979	11	0
1980	8	3
1981	2	9
1982	2	9
1983	9	2
1984	11	0
1985	N/A	N/A
1986	N/A	N/A
1987	N/A	N/A
1988	4	7
1989	8	3
1990	5	6
1991	3	8

Coach McDonald's
Blue Mound High School Basketball Teams

1964   Junior Varsity

Kim Brown
Kent Gorden
Phil Brown
Jay Brown
Jerry Logue   18 – 0   J.V.
Gene Giles   2 – 0   Frosh
Chuck Plunkett   2 – 0   Fr-So

Tourney
Don Naber
Gene Pistorius
Sam Sloan
Dan Hutton
David McVey

Cheerleaders

JV	Varsity
Karen Kornewald	Cheryl Hobbs
Sue Garrison	Brenda Thiele
Betty Etherton	Judy Carr
Jean Boggs	Rita Bailey
Dorrine Ryan	Marnie Bankson
Mascot = Kim Miller	

1965   Junior Varsity   12 W – 6 L

Mike Damery
Bill Augustine
Sam Pate
Sam Sloan
David McVey
Kirk Sunderland
John Brown

Randy Carr
Don Ferguson
John Ferguson
Jim Weybright
Pete Bankson
Kent Gorden
Phil Brown
Bill Clark
John Pistorius
Kim Brown
Ken Huffman
Cheerleaders

JV	**Varsity**
Peggy Rainey	Jean Boggs
Cathy Canady	Diana Damery
Sue Chapman	Sue Garrison
Sharon Nelson	Beverly Pistorius
Sheila Oxford	Roberta Wilcox
Mascot = Kim Miller	

1966   Junior Varsity   13 W – 5 L

David Noland
Leon Pruett
Doug Hadden
Kirk Sunderland
Lane Traughber
Bill Augustine
Guy O'Bryan
Dean Sefried
Mike Maulding
Bevin Aufrecht
Jim Weybright
Dan Green
Gail Edmunds
Mike Damery
Rick Lowe
Bob Clark

1966   Varsity Team   21 W – 8 L

*Denotes Varsity Letter Winner

- *Pete Bankson
- *Kim Brown
- *Jay Brown   Capt.
- *Paul Sperry   MVP, Roger Uhll Free Throw Award
- John Brown
- *Gene Giles
- *Bill Clark
- Phil Brown
- Kent Gorden
- *Dan Hutton
- Ken Huffman

Volunteer Coach: Bill Meyers

Cheerleaders

JV	Varsity
Sharon Nelson	Sue Garrison
Roberta Wilcox	Beverly Pistorius
Cathy Canady	Marcy Heller
Sue Chapman	Diana Damery
Beverly Pistorius	Jean Boggs

1967   Varsity Team   14 W – 9 L

*Denotes Varsity Letter Winner

- *Guy O'Bryan
- *Pete Bankson
- *Kim Brown   MVP, Roger Uhll Free Throw Award
- David Noland
- Gail Edmunds
- *Kirk Sunderland
- Doug Hadden
- *John Pistorius
- John Brown
- *Phil Brown   Capt.
- *Kent Gorden
- *Ken Huffman

Volunteer Coach: Bill Meyers

Cheerleaders

JV	Varsity
Sharon Nelson	Diana Damery
Patricia Buzan	Marcy Heller
Lynnette Brown	Judy Woodcock
Cathy Canaday	Becky Brown
Beverly Pistorius	Jan Garrison

1968   Varsity Team   15 W – 10 L

*Denotes Varsity Letter Winner

*Gail Edmunds

*Doug Hadden

Dan Green

*John Pistorius   Capt., Most Rebounds, Roger
Uhll Free Throw Award

Lane Traughber

*Kirk Sunderland

Trent Wilcox

Dan Robinson

*Eric Thiele

*Tom Ritter

*Pete Bankson   MVP

*Ken Huffman

Assistant Coach: Art Newton

Cheerleaders

JV	Varsity
Debbie Vincent	Judy Woodcock
Linda Botoner	Marcy Heller
Patricia Sperry	Becky Brown
Alice Bean	Jan Garrison
Lynnette Damery	Patricia Buzan

Statisticians

Susie Albers

Nancy Cook

1969   Varsity Team   18 W – 8 L

*Denotes Varsity Letter Winner

- Stan Henderson
- *Dale Usinger
- *Dan Robinson
- *Tom Younker
- *Brent Damery
- *Dan Green
- *Gail Edmunds   Capt., Most Rebounds
- *Tom Ritter   MVP
- *Eric Thiele   Roger Uhll Free Throw Award
- Paul Gorden

Assistant Coach: Joe Zimmerman

Cheerleaders

JV	Varsity
Diane Lowe	Debbie Vincent
Laneva Henderson	Linda Botoner
Patricia Sperry	Janet Nelson
Lynette Botoner	Debbie Shaffer
Rhonda Crow	Lynnette Damery

Statisticians

- Carolyn Hill
- Susan Meisenhelter

1970   Varsity Team   23 W – 4 L

*Denotes Varsity Letter Winner

- John Heller
- Kent Hadden
- *Tom Ritter   Capt.
- *Tom Younker   MVP, Roger Uhll Free Throw Award
- *Dan Robinson
- *Brent Damery   Most Rebounds, Most Improved
- *Dale Usinger   Best Defensive
- *Stan Henderson
- *John Bonn
- *Paul Gorden

Assistant Coach: Joe Zimmerman

Cheerleaders
  Debbie Vincent
  Linda Botoner
  Patricia Sperry
  Laneva Henderson
  Linda Younker
  Lynnette Botoner
Statisticians
  Carolyn Hill
  Ramona Chapman
  Kathy Meisenhelter

1971   Varsity Team   16 W – 7 L
*Denotes Varsity Letter Winner
  *John Heller
  Stan Henderson
  Dennis Younker
  Mike Oxby
  Richard Ritter
  Dennis Kraft
  Greg Thiele
  Greg Mathias
  *Tom Younker   Roger Uhll Free Throw Award,
  *Dale Usinger   Capt., MVP, Most Rebounds
  *Paul Gorden
  *Brent Damery
  *Kent Hadden
Assistant Coach: Gary Stevenson
Cheerleaders
  LaNeva Henderson
  Diane Noland
  Lynette Botoner
  Diane Lowe
  Debbie Showalter
  Linda Younker
  Mascot / Marcy McDonald

Statisticians
> Ramona Chapman
> M'Liss Huffman
> Janet Mercer

1972   Did Not Coach

1973   Varsity Team   12 W – 12 L

*Denotes Varsity Letter Winner

*Duane Noland	Best Defensive
Rodney Damery	
*Randy Damery	
*Dennis Younker	MVP
*Tom Pistorius	
*Dave Pistorius	Roger Uhll Free Throw Award, Most Rebounds
Steve Kraus	
*Kevin Burns	
*Richard Ritter	Best Hustler
*Mike Oxby	Capt.
Doug Fitzgerald	
*Tim Armstrong	Most Improved

Assistant Coaches: Gary Stevenson, Pete Manhart

Cheerleaders

JV	Varsity
Peggy Woodcock	Linda Younker
Janet Gaither	Diane Noland
Denise Ryan	Jan Minks
Michelle Lewis	Terri Logue
Teresa Brown	Debbie Showalter

Statisticians
> Tina Beckett
> Debbie Drysdale
> Cathy Meisenhelter
> Diana Virt
> Tami Clark

1974   Varsity Team   21 W – 6 L

*Denotes Varsity Letter Winner

*Duane Noland	Best Defensive
*Tim Armstrong	Capt.
*Kevin Burns	
*Tom Pistorius	
*Randy Damery	Best Hustler
Rodney Damery	
Mike Bourisaw	
*David Pistorius	MVP, Most Reb., Roger Uhll Free Throw Award
*Steve Kraus	Most Improved
Dick Martin	
*Dan Byard	

Assistant Coaches: Gary Stevenson, Pete Manhart

Cheerleaders

JV	**Varsity**
Beth Meador	Jan Minks
Joyce White	Terri Logue
Julie Garrison	Peggy Woodcock
Diane Gilpin	Janet Gaither
Della Ryan	Teresa Brown

Statisticians

Cathy Meisenhelter
Debbie Drysdale
Diana Virt
Tami Clark
Tina Beckett

1975   Varsity Team   24 W – 2 L

*Denotes Varsity Letter Winner

*Dan Byard	Capt., Best Defensive, Most Assists
*Steve Kraus	
*David Pistorius	MVP, Most Reb., All Conf., Roger Uhll Free Throw Award
*Mike Bourisaw	
*Rodney Damery	
David Scales	

*Ed Bailey	Best Hustler, Most Improved
*Gary Jackson	All Conference
Tim Rainey	
Jim Nolen	
Ken Gilpin	
Kent Kraus	
Brian Robinson	

Assistant Coaches: Gary Stevenson, Pete Manhart

Cheerleaders

JV	Varsity
Rita Canady	Joyce White
Renee Damery	Diana Gilpin
Julie Garrison	Terri Logue
Phillis Seitz	Janet Gaither
Beth Meador	Teresa Brown

Statisticians

Tami Clark
Renae Sperry
Lori Gordon
Diana Virt
Debi Clark
Julie Buzan

1976   Varsity Team   18 W – 8 L

*Denotes Varsity Letter Winner

*Ken Gilpin	
Mike Jackson	
Brian Robinson	
*Kelly Armstrong	
Dale Byard	
Tim Allen	
*Mark Houser	
*Brad Eckols	
*Gary Jackson	MVP, Macon Co Tourn. MVP, Most Rebounds, All Conf., Roger Uhll Free Throw Award
*Tim Rainey	All Conf., Most Improved
*Ed Bailey	Capt., Best Defensive, Best Hustler

*David Scales
Assistant Coaches: Gary Stevenson, Pete Manhart
Cheerleaders

JV	Varsity
Suzi Allen	Teresa Brown
Phyllis Seitz	Diana Gilpin
Carol Gilpin	Rita Canada
Dena Virt	Renee Damery
Marcelle Lewis	Julie Garrison

Statisticians
Diana Virt
Tami Clark
Janice Drysdale
Debi Clark
Julie Buzan
Lori Gordon

1977 Varsity Team 27 W – 1 L

*Denotes Varsity Letter Winner

Doug Collier
Todd Logue
Dale Byard
Tom Dalluge
*Kelly Armstrong
*Tim Rainey   All Conference
*David Scales
*Mark Houser   All Conf., Best Defensive, Most
                     Imp., Most Rebounds
*Brad Eckols
*Gary Jackson   All Conf., MVP, Roger Uhll Free
                     Throw Award
*Ed Bailey   Capt., All Conf., Best Def., Best
                     Hustler, Most Assists

Assistant Coach: Phil Baca

Cheerleaders
JV
Cheryl Huffman
Carol Jackson
Suzi Allen
Dena Virt
Carol Gilpin
Statisticians
Dani Meador
Veda Elder
Susan Flamm
Betty Garner
Lori Gordon
Julie Buzan

Varsity
Diana GIlpin
Julie Garrison
Renee Damery
Marcelle Lewis
Rita Canaday

1978   Varsity Team   26 W – 1 L

*Denotes Varsity Letter Winner
Dennis Noland
*Doug Collier
Dale Byard
Jim Brown
*Bill Younger
*David Scales
*Brad Eckols   MVP, Roger Uhll Free Throw Award, Most Rebounds

Mike Peer
*Kelly Armstrong   Capt., Most Assists
*Mike Jackson
*Todd Logue
Rick Brown
Tod Nicholls
Assistant Coach: Phil Baca
Cheerleaders
JV
Carol Jackson
Debbie Hall
Laurie Sturgis

Varsity
Cheryl Huffman
Renee Damery
Rita Canady

Cathy Gilpin
Carol Gilpin

Dena Virt
Marcelle Lewis

Statisticians
Melanie Ward
Dani Meador
Betty Garner
Susan Flamm
Julie Buzan
Lori Gordon

1979   **Varsity Team**   **19 W – 7 L**

*Denotes Varsity Letter Winner

*Doug Collier	MVP, Tri-Capt., Most Rebounds
*Todd Logue	Tri-Captain, Most Assists
*Mike Jackson	Tri-Capt., Roger Uhll Free Throw Award

*Bill Younger
*Rick Brown
*Jim Brown
Tod Nicholls
Mike Peer
Dennis Noland
Ben Tucker
Joe Crump
Todd Brown
Steve Williams
Chris Usinger
Bill True

Assistant Coach: Phil Baca

Cheerleaders

JV	**Varsity**
Carol Jackson	Marcelle Lewis
Gena Lewis	Dena VIrt
Debbie Hall	Cheryl Huffman
Vicki Brownlee	Kristie King
	Laurie Sturgis

Statisticians

Melanie Ward
Julie Bonham
Crystal Tullis
Susan Flamm
Debbie Chapman

1980   Varsity Team   19 W – 7 L

*Denotes Varsity Letter Winner

*Tod Nicholls	Capt., Best Hustler, Most Assists
*Ben Tucker	
*Joe Crump	
*Steve Williams	Most Improved
*Chris Usinger	Most Rebounds
*Jim Brown	
Steve Miller	
*Bill True	
Steve Scales	
*Bill Younger	All Conference, MVP, Roger Uhll Free Throw Award
*Dennis Noland	Best Defensive
Trent Logue	
Scott Woolever	

Assistant Coach: Phil Baca

Cheerleaders

JV	Varsity
Cathy Gilpin	Carol Jackson
Karen Brown	Laurie Sturgis
Michelle Tucker	Kristie King
Jill Wubben	Vicki Brownlee
Teresa Rhodemann	Cheryl Morr

Statisticians
Cheryl Drysdale
Crystal Tullis
Melanie Ward
Debbie Chapman
Julie Bonham
Tina Hite

1981   Varsity Team   5W – 18L

*Denotes Varsity Letter Winner

Brian Damery	
*Bill True	Capt, MVP, Roger Uhll Free Throw Award
*Chris Usinger	Best Defensive, Most Rebounds
*Steve Williams	
*Chris Parsons	
Bruce Bailey	
Jim Elder	
Pete Gilson	
*Georger Booker	
*Mike Collier	
*Steve Miller	Most Assists
*Brent Doyle	
*Trent Logue	Best Hustler, Most Improved

Assistant Coach: Phil Baca

Cheerleaders

JV	Varsity
Annette Younker	Cheryl Morr
Diana Koonce	Jill Wubben
Janet Walters	Teresa Rhodemann
Marcy McDonald	Wendy Sattler
LeAnn Thiele	Michelle Tucker

Statisticians

Cheryl Drysdale
Sherry Flamm
Julie Bonham
Crystal Tullis
Lisa Cox
Tina Hite

1982   Varsity Team   8 W – 17 L

*Denotes Varsity Letter Winner

Eric Brown
Eddie Morr
*Mike Wilhoit

*Brian Damery
*Bruce Bailey
*Chris Parsons   Most Rebounds
Tony Cooper
Jim Elder
Mike Gorden
*Mike Collier   MVP, Roger Uhll Award
*George Booker   Best Defensive, Best Hustler
Pete Gilson
*Trent Logue   Capt.
*Mladen Matisa   Most Improved
Jeff Hadden
Assistant Coach: Phil Baca

Cheerleaders

JV	Varisty
Teresa Rhodemann	Cheryl Morr
Jill Wubben	Marcy McDonald
Joanie Dillon	LeAnn Thiele
Nikki Goad	Annette Younker
Christy Sarver	Michelle Tucker

Statisticians
Sue Wubben
Tina Hite
Sherry Flamm
Vicki Wilhoit
Gretchen Damery
Cheryl Drysdale
Lisa Cox

1983   Varsity Team   20 W – 9 L

*Denotes Varsity Letter Winner
Bob Koonce
*George Booker   Best Defensive, Best Hustler
*Mike Collier   All Conf., Capt., Roger Uhll Free
                    Throw Award, Most Assists

Eric Brown
Brad Damery
Pete Gilson

*Mike Wilhoit
*Brian Damery
*Chris Parsons   All Conference, MVP, Most
                         Rebounds
*Bruce Bailey   Most Improved
*Eddie Morr
Matt Sefried
Assistant Coach: Phil Baca

Cheerleaders

JV	Varsity
Diana Koonce	LeAnn Thiele
Christy Sarver	Marcy McDonald
Nikki Goad	Annette Younker
Katie Anderson	Jill Wubben

Statisticians

Tina Hite
Lisa Sattler
Gretchen Damery
Erin Franklin
Tammy Brown
Sue Wubben
Cheryl Drysdale

1984 Varsity Team   26 W – 2 L

*Denotes Varsity Letter Winner

*Eric Brown   Most Improved, Roger Uhll Free
                        Throw Award
*Eddie Morr   Most Assists (tie)
*Tony Cooper
*Bruce Bailey
*Chris Parsons   All Conference, MVP
*Mike Wilhoit
Bob Koonce
Brad Damery
*Mike Collier   All Conf., Capt., Best Def., Best
                        Hustler, Most Assists (tie)
Matt Sefried
Larry Wilderman

Corry Garren
*Pete Gilson
Assistant Coach: Phil Baca

Cheerleaders

JV	Varsity
Tina Gunnels	Annette Younker
Aundrea Sefried	Marcy McDonald
Debbie Brownlee	LeAnn Thiele
Lori Parsons	Diana Koonce
Noelle Carr	Rochelle Walters

Statisticians
Geri Sattler
Katie Anderson
Sue Wubben
Tammy Brown
Erin Franklin
Gretchen Damery

1985　　　**Did Not Coach**

1986　　　**Did Not Coach**

1987　　　**Did Not Coach**

1988 Varsity Team　8 W – 16 L

*Denotes Varsity Letter Winner
　*Brandon Housh
　*Travis Southard
　Jay Weaver
　*Matt Parsons
　*Scott Jewsbury　　Capt., MVP, Roger Uhll Free Throw Award, Conf. 1st Team, Macon County Team

　*Kevin Evans　　Most Improved, Most Rebounds
　*Chris Moomey
　Greg Giberson
　*Eric Pistorius　　Best Defensive

Bruce Jones
*Chad Jones   Best Hustler, Most Assists
Brian Jones
Assistant Coach: Randy Newton
Cheerleaders
　JV   **Varsity**
　Consuelo Etherton   Rhonda Damery
　Angela Duster   Michelle Damery
　Heidi Richardson   Carrie Marshall
                                 Kathy Jackson
                                 Carrie Scott

Statisticians
　Karen Karraker
　Darlene Hicks
　April Colton
　Jodi Holmgren
　Tricia Sargeant
　Kari Wetzel

1989 　　**Varsity Team** 　　**16 W – 11 L**
*Denotes Varsity Letter Winner
　*Bruce Jones
　Kent Hoffman
　*Chris Moomey
　*Kevin Evans   Most Improved, Most Rebounds
　*Scott Jewsbury   Capt., MVP, Best Def. (tie), All
                          Conf., All County, Roger Uhll Free
                          Throw Award

　Jeff Brown
　Jason Brown
　*Brandon Housh   Best Hustler
　*Travis Southard
　*Eric Pistorius   Best Defensive (tie)
　*Matt Parsons
　*Brian Jones
Assistant Coach: Randy Newton

Cheerleaders

JV	Varsity
Stacey White	Lisa Hull
Kim Arends	Rhonda Damery
Mary Kirk	Heidi Richardson
Dottie Scott	Consuelo Etherton
Shelly Lynch	

Statisticians
Kari Wetzel
Karen Karraker
Kathy Jackson
Jill Pistorius
Alice Smith
Tricia Sargeant

1990   Varsity Team   W – 12 L

*Denotes Varsity Letter Winner

*George Meisenhelter	Best Hustler
Shane Thrasher	Most Improved
Pete Pistorius	
Jeff Bonn	
Coery Lines	
*Eric Pistorius	Capt., Best Defensive
*Jason Brown	
*Jeff Brown	Most Assists
*Kevin Evans	MVP, All Conference, All County, Most Rebounds
*Kent Hoffman	
John Richardson	
Jared Hopkins	
*Brandon Housh	

Assistant Coach: Randy Newton

Cheerleaders
Cory Johnson
Shelle Fansler
Mary Kirk
Heidi Richardson
Kathy Jackson

Statisticians
Jennifer Turner
Sarah Hill
Karen Karraker
Jill Pistorius
Kari Wetzel
Alice Smith

1991   Varsity Team   4 W – 18 L

*Denotes Varsity Letter Winner
Russell Knaus
*Cory Lines
Jason Smith
*Chris Scott
Nathan Damery
*Jeff Bonn
*Pete Pistorius   Best Hustler (tie)
*Jared Hopkins   Best Defensive
*Jeff Brown
*Jason Brown   MVP, Capt., Roger Uhll Free Throw Award

*George Meisenhelter   Best Hustler (tie), Most Improved

Assistant Coach: Steve Berg
Cheerleaders

JV	Varsity
Sally Tish	Dottie Scott
Shelly Verhusen	Mary Kirk
Sarah Hill	Cory Johnson
Tiffany Wetzel	Heidi Richardson
Jamie Wilkin	Kara Toney

Statisticians (Inc.)
Jill Pistorius
Alice Smith
Kari Wetze

Basketball Award Winners
During Coach McDonald's Career

1966

MVP	Paul Sperry	
CAPT.	Jay Brown	
Roger Uhll Free Throw Award	Paul Sperry	80.5%

1967

MVP	Kim Brown	
CAPT.	Phil Brown	
Roger Uhll Free Throw Award	Kim Brown	83.3%

1968

MVP	Pete Bankson	
CAPT.	John Pistorius	
Roger Uhll Free Throw Award	John Pistorius	74.3%
Most Rebounds	John Pistorius	141

1969

MVP	Tom Ritter	
CAPT.	Gail Edmunds	
Roger Uhll Free Throw Award	Eric Thiele	75.0%
Most Rebounds	Gail Edmunds	179

1970

MVP	Tom Younker	
CAPT.	Tom Ritter	
Roger Uhll Free Throw Award	Tom Younker	78.2%
Most Rebounds	Brent Damery	217
Most Improved Player	Brent Damery	
Best Defensive Player	Dale Usinger	

1971

MVP	Dale Usinger	
CAPT.	Dale Usinger	

| Roger Uhll Free Throw Award | Tom Younker | 86.8% |
| Most Rebounds | Dale Usinger | 205 |

1972   DID NOT COACH

1973
MVP	Dennis Younker	
CAPT.	Mike Oxby	
Roger Uhll Free Throw Award	David Pistorius	74.1%
Most Rebounds	David Pistorius	159
Most Improved Player	Tim Armstrong	
Best Defensive Player	Duane Noland	
Hustler Award	Richard Ritter	

1974
MVP	David Pistorius	
CAPT.	Tim Armstrong	
Roger Uhll Free Throw Award	David Pistorius	78.5%
Most Rebounds	David Pistorius	165
Most Improved Player	Steve Kraus	
Best Defensive Player	Duane Noland	
Hustler Award	Randy Damery	
Most Assists	Tim Armstrong	141

1975
MVP	David Pistorius	
CAPT.	Danny Byard	
Roger Uhll Free Throw Award	David Pistorius	84.0%
Most Rebounds	David Pistorius	209
Most Improved Player	Ed Bailey	
Best Defensive Player	Danny Byard	
Hustler Award	Ed Bailey	
Most Assists	Danny Byard	220
All Conference	David Pistorius	
	Gary Jackson	

1976

MVP	Gary Jackson	
CAPT.	Ed Bailey	
Roger Uhll Free Throw Award	Gary Jackson	86.8%
Most Rebounds	Gary Jackson	220
Most Improved Player	Tim Rainey	
Best Defensive Player	Ed Bailey	
Hustler Award	Ed Bailey	
All Conference	Gary Jackson	
	Tim Rainey	

1977

MVP	Gary Jackson	
CAPT.	Ed Bailey	
Roger Uhll Free Throw Award	Gary Jackson	90.7%
Most Rebounds	Mark Houser	199
Most Improved	Mark Houser	
Best Defensive	Ed Bailey	
Hustler	Ed Bailey	
Most Assists	Ed Bailey	106
All Conference	Gary Jackson	
	Ed Bailey	
	Mark Houser	
	Tim Rainey	

1978

MVP	Brad Eckols	
CAPT.	Kelly Armstrong	
Roger Uhll Free Throw Award	Brad Eckols	78.0%
Most Rebounds	Brad Eckols	189
Most Assists	Kelly Armstrong	139

1979

MVP	Doug Collier	
TRI- CAPTAINS	Doug Collier	
	Mike Jackson	
	Todd Logue	
Roger Uhll Free Throw Award	Mike Jackson	83.3%
Most Rebounds	Doug Collier	192
Most Assists	Todd Logue	168

1980

MVP	Bill Younger	
CAPT.	Tod Nicholls	
Roger Uhll Free Throw Award	Bill Younger	78.6%
Most Rebounds	Chris Usinger	186
Most Improved Player	Steve Williams	
Best Defensive Player	Dennis Noland	
Hustler Award	Tod Nicholls	
Most Assists	Tod Nicholls	N/A

1981

MVP	Bill True	
CAPT.	Bill True	
Roger Uhll Free Throw Award	Bill True	82.0%
Most Rebounds	Chris Usinger	218
Most Improved Player	Trent Logue	
Best Defensive Player	Chris Usinger	
Hustler	Trent Logue	
Most Assists	Steve Miller	65

1982

MVP	Mike Collier	
CAPT.	Trent Logue	
Roger Uhll Free Throw Award	Mike Collier	60.8%
Most Rebounds	Chris Parsons	196
Most Improved Player	Mladen Matisa	
Best Defensive	George Booker	

Hustler Award	George Booker	
Most Assists	Trent Logue	84

1983

MVP	Chris Parsons	
CAPT.	Mike Collier	
Roger Uhll Free Throw Award	Mike Collier	71.7%
Most Rebounds	Chris Parsons	291
Most Improved Player	Bruce Bailey	
Best Defensive	George Booker	
Hustler Award	George Booker	
Most Assists	Mike Collier	124

1984

MVP	Chris Parsons	
CAPT.	Mike Collier	
Roger Uhll Free Throw Award	Eric Brown	72.5%
Most Rebounds	Chris Parsons	239
Most Improved Player	Eric Brown	
Best Defensive	Mike Collier	
Hustler Award	Mike Collier	
Most Assists	Mike Collier	91
	Eddie Morr	91

1985   DID NOT COACH

1986   DID NOT COACH

1987   DID NOT COACH

1988

MVP	Scott Jewsberry	
CAPT.	Scott Jewsberry	
Roger Uhll Free Throw Award	Scott Jewsberry	75.5%
Most Rebounds	Kevin Evans	181

Most Improved Player	Kevin Evans	
Best Defensive Player	Eric Pistorius	
Hustler Award	Chad Jones	
Most Assists	Chad Jones	108

1989

MVP	Scott Jewsberry	
CAPT.	Scott Jewsberry	
Roger Uhll Free Throw Award	Scott Jewsberry	80.9%
Most Rebounds	Kevin Evans	235
Most Improved Player	Kevin Evans	
Best Defensive	Scott Jewsberry	
	Eric Pistorius	
Hustler Award	Brandon Housh	

1990

MVP	Kevin Evans	
CAPT.	Eric Pistorius	
Most Rebounds	Kevin Evans	261
Most Improved Player	Shane Thrasher	
Best Defensive	Eric Pistorius	
Hustler Award	George Meisenhelter	
Most Assists	Jeff Brown	78

1991

MVP	Jason Brown	
CAPT.	Jason Brown	
Most Improved Player	George Meisenhelter	
Best Defensive	Jared Hopkins	
Hustler Award	Pete Pistorius	
	George Meisenhelter	
Roger Uhll Free Throw Award	Jason Brown	66.3%

Note: The Roger Uhll Free Throw Award was awarded to the player who had the best free-throw percentage with a minimum of 50 free throw attempts.

Note: The information in this section came mostly from high school yearbooks. Every effort has been made to correctly represent the awards given; however, some information was unavailable. Apologies go out to those people who are not properly represented here.

Scott Jewsbury, 3rd in scoring for Blue Mound High School. Picture from the 1989 yearbook.

Specific Record Holders
During Coach McDonald's Career

Best Free-Throw Percentage in a Season with a 50 Attempt Minimum

Gary Jackson   1976-77   88 made of 96 attempts   91.7%

Most Assists in One Season

Tod Nicholls   1979-80   224

Most Rebounds in a Season

Chris Parsons   1982-83   291

Most Points in One Season

David Pistorius   1974-75   703

Most Points in One Game   (Including 3-Point Field-Goals)

Scott Jewsbury   vs. Argenta-Oreana @ A/O   2/2/88   43 pts.

Most Points in One Game

Gary Jackson   vs. Macon @ Blue Mound   1/10/75 41 pts.

Coach McDonald's Players Who Achieved 500+ Career Points

1966	Paul Sperry	1032
	Gene Giles	605
1967	Kim Brown	619
1968	Pete Bankson	590
1970	Tom Ritter	761
1971	Tom Younker	1000
	Dale Usinger	944
*1972	Brent Damery	1180
1975	David Pistorius	1736
1977	Gary Jackson	1869
	Ed Bailey	913
	Tim Rainey	866
1978	David Scales	921
	Brad Eckols	699
1979	Doug Collier	877
	Mike Jackson	845
	Todd Logue	730
1980	Bill Younger	1001
	Jim Brown	516
1981	Steve Williams	694

1984	Mike Collier	1386
	Chris Parsons	1256
	Bruce Bailey	677
*1985	Eddie Morr	1240
*1986	Bob Koonce	559
1987	Kevin Evans	797
	Jeff Lasowski	796
	Jeff Brown	770
	Tim White	642
1989	Scott Jewsbury	1400
1990	Kevin Evans	1317
	Eric Pistorius	1020
1991	Jason Brown	537

*Note:
Coach McDonald did not coach in the following years: 1972, 1985, 1986, 1987.
However, the players listed above played on McDonald's teams in prior years

Other Players from Blue Mound
Who Achieved 500+ Points in Their Career
(All of these players played for Coach Bob Miller)

1960	David Brown	973 pts.
	Bob Ritter	594 pts.
1961	Phil Damery	510 pts.
1962	Norman Moss	914 pts.
1964	Bob Albers	693 pts.
	Allan Snyder	656 pts.
	Ron Naber	518 pts.
1965	Jerry Heller	795 pts.

1000 Point Club

The following players for Coach McDonald achieved 1000+ points during their high school career at Blue Mound High School:

1.	1869 pts.	Gary Jackson	Class of 1977
2.	1736 pts.	David Pistorius	Class of 1975
3.	*1400 pts.	Scott Jewsbury	Class of 1989
4.	1386 pts.	Mike Collier	Class of 1984
5.	*1317 pts.	Kevin Evans	Class of 1990
6.	1256 pts.	Chris Parsons	Class of 1984
7.	1240 pts.	Eddie Morr	Class of 1985
8.	1180 pts.	Brent Damery	Class of 1972
9.	*1146 pts.	Jared Hopkins	Class of 1993
10.	1032 pts.	Paul Sperry	Class of 1966
11.	*1020 pts.	Eric Pistorius	Class of 1990
12.	1001 pts.	Bill Younger	Class of 1980
13.	1000 pts.	Tom Younker	Class of 1971

* Denotes 3-point shot inclusion.

Note: There were 2 other players in Blue Mound history who reached career totals of 1000+ points. These players played for Coach Bob Miller.

Terry Coffman   1274 pts.   Class of 1961
Terry Rainey   1051 pts.   Class of 1965

#1 and #2 Scorers in Blue Mound History

Gary Jackson
*The All-Time Leading Scorer
 in Blue Mound History
*1869 career points.
*Macon Co. Tourney MVP
 1976 & 1977
*2013 Candidate for High
 School Hall of Fame

David Pistorius
*1974 & 1975 Macon County
 Tourney MVP
*2nd in Scoring at BMHS
*1736 Career Points
*2012 Hall of Fame Player
*Member of Millikin
 University Hall of Fame

   *Note: Jackson's total includes 236 varsity points scored at Niantic-Harristown High School during his freshman year. Jackson's total varsity points for his 3 years at Blue Mound is 1633, which is 8 points higher than Pistorius's total for his last 3 years of high school.

Assistant Basketball Coaches

1966	Bill Meyers
1967	Bill Meyers
1968	Art Newton
1969	Joe Zimmerman
1970	Joe Zimmerman
1971	Gary Stevenson
1972	DID NOT COACH
1973	Pete Manhart / Gary Stevenson
1974	Pete Manhart / Gary Stevenson
1975	Pete Manhart / Gary Stevenson
1976	Pete Manhart / Gary Stevenson
1977	Phil Baca
1978	Phil Baca
1979	Phil Baca
1980	Phil Baca
1981	Phil Baca
1982	Phil Baca
1983	Phil Baca
1984	Phil Baca
1985	DID NOT COACH
1986	DID NOT COACH
1987	DID NOT COACH
1988	Randy Newton
1989	Randy Newton
1990	Randy Newton
1991	Steve Berg

Official Scorers

1966	Robert "Peck" Wilcox
1967	Robert "Peck" Wilcox
1968	Robert "Peck" Wilcox
1969	Robert "Peck" Wilcox
1970	Charlie Cawthon
1971	Charlie Cawthon
1972	Did Not Coach
1973	Charlie Cawthon
1974	Charlie Cawthon
1975	Charlie Cawthon
1976	Charlie Cawthon
1977	Charlie Cawthon
1978	Charlie Cawthon
1979	Charlie Cawthon
1980	Charlie Cawthon
1981	Stan Otto
1982	Stan Otto
1983	Stan Otto
1984	Stan Otto
1985	Did Not Coach
1986	Did Not Coach
1987	Did Not Coach
1987	Did Not Coach
1988	Kathy Newton
1989	Kathy Newton
1990	Kathy Newton
1991	Unavailable

Official Timer

George Bricker was the Official Timer from 1966 – 1991. He was inducted into the Illinois Basketball Coaches Hall of Fame as a Friend of Basketball in 1993.

Vic Oxby was a substitute timer.

Basketball Managers

1966	David Holtfreter
1967	Jim Batman / John Harlin
1968	Mark Whitten / John Kendall
1969	Steve White / Bill Beck
1970	Bill Beck / Werner Leigel
1971	Bill Beck
1972	DID NOT COACH
1973	Jim Bos / Bill Beck
1975	Doug Fitzgerald
1976	David Clark
1977	Harry Crump
1978	Mark Woodcock
1979	Not Available
1980	Not Available
1981	Not Available
1982	Todd Klay / Scott Damery
1983	Todd Klay
1984	Jeff Brown
1985	DID NOT COACH
1986	DID NOT COACH
1987	DID NOT COACH
1988	Leon Parton
1989	Oscar Crowe
1990	Not Available
1991	Not Available

TRACK

Coach McDonald served as the boys' track coach from 1966 through the 1979 season. In his 13 year career, McDonald and the Knights won an impressive 37 championships including 9 consecutive years as the Meridian Conference Champions from 1971 to 1979. McDonald coached the Knights to 7 Arthur Invitational championships, 5 Macon County Championships, and 4 District Championships. The Knights also won the Cerro Gordo Invitational 3 times and the Pana Open twice during McDonald's run as coach.

McDonald was named the *Decatur Herald and Review* "Coach of the Year" in 1971, 1976, 1977, and 1979. From 1977 to 1979 McDonald and his Knights brought home 6 State Meet medals:

1977	Mark Houser	6th place	Triple Jump
1977	Doug Collier	3rd place	2-Mile Relay
	Bart Tucker		
	David Scales		
	Mike Jackson		
1978	David Scales	5th place	880 Yd. Run
1978	Mike Jackson	4th place	330 Yd. Low Hurdles
1978	Mike Jackson	1st place	880 Yd. Run
1979	Mike Jackson	1st place	880 Yd. Run

Year	Championships Won
1966	
1967	
1968	
1969	
1970	
1971	
	Arthur Invitational
	Macon County
	Meridian Conference
	Cerro Gordo Invitational
1972	
	Meridian Conference
	Cerro Gordo Invitational
	Arthur Invitational
1973	
	Meridian Conference
1974	
	Meridian Conference
	Arthur Invitational
1975	
	Meridian Conference Fr./So.
	Meridian Conference
	Cerro Gordo Invitational
1976	
	Macon County
	Arthur Invitational
	Pana Open
	Meridian Conference Fr./So.
	Meridian Conference
	District
1977	
	Pana Open
	Macon County

	Arthur Invitational
	Meridian Conference Fr./So.
	Meridian Conference
	District
1978	
	Pana Open
	Macon County
	Arthur Invitational
	Meridian Conference Fr./So.
	Meridian Conference
	District
1979	
	Chatham-Glenwood Invitational
	Macon County
	Arthur Invitational
	Meridian Conference
	Macon County
	District Co-Champions

Track Records During Coach McDonald's Era

Event	Athlete	Result	Year
100 yd dash	Doug Fitzgerald	9.9	1974
	Scott Armstrong	9.9	1976
220 yd. dash	Scott Armstrong	21.7	1976
180 Low Hurdles	Paul Gorden	20.9	1971
440 yd. dash	Mike Jackson	50.3	1978
880 yd run	Mike Jackson	1:53.57	1979
Mile Run	Frank Bailey	4:32.4	1973
Two Mile Run	Ed Bailey	10:09	1977
High Hurdles	Mike Jackson	14.5	1979
Low Hurdles	Mike Jackson	37.75	1978
High Jump	Jim Nolen	6'4"	1977
Pole Vault	Jeff Zeeb	11'6"	1972
	Doug Collier	11'6"	1979
Shot Put	Bill Younger	52'6.5"	1979
*Discus	Bill Younger	140'2"	1979
*Triple Jump	Mark Houser	43'9.5"	1977
Long Jump	David Pistorius	21'10"	1975

440 yd. Relay	Doug Fitzgerald Randy Damery Scott Armstrong Duane Noland	45.0	1974
440 yd Frosh Relay	Greg Thiele Ken Ervin Dell McCoy Brent Damery	49.4	1969
880 yd. Relay	Paul Gorden Dale Usinger Dell McCoy Brent Damery	1:36	1971
Mile Relay	Rick Brown David Scales Doug Collier Mike Jackson	3:26.5	1978
2 Mile Relay	Doug Collier David Scales Bart Tucker Mike Jackson	7:59.6	1977

*Note:
Two new records were set after Coach McDonald retired.

Discus	Bill Younger	145'7.5"	1980
Triple Jump	Steve Williams	44'10"	1981

1978 State Track Meet: Mike Jackson receiving 1ˢᵗ place in the 880 yd. run and David Scales earning 5ᵗʰ place.

Note: David Scales blistered his feet during the preliminary round and still ran in the final, placing 5ᵗʰ. He is pictured here on the Winner's Podium in his bare feet.

Track Teams

1966 / Team Members

Gene Giles Co-Captain	Jack Eson
Dan Hutton	Mike Shaffer
Leon Zeeb	John Lewis
Greg Armstrong	Joe Murphy
Rick Hadden Co-Captain	Merle Brown
Kim Brown	Mike Scales
John McVey	Lane Traughber
David McVey	Joe Widner
Bill Clark	Terry Patient
Richard Canaday	Leon Wellwood
Guy O'Bryan	
Phil Brown	
David Cook	
Larry Hicks	
Assistant Coach	**Bill Meyers**
Manager	**David Holtfreter**

Coach McDonald's First Track Team. (1966)
Picture taken from the Blue Mound High School yearbook

Row One: Coach McDonald, David Cook, Leon Zeeb, Gene Giles, Larry Hicks, Greg Armstrong, Dan Hutton.
Row Two: Mr. Meyers, Kim Brown, Phil Brown, Leon Wellwood, Rick Hadden, Jack Eason, Mike Shaffer.
Row Three: John Lewis, Joe Murphy, Merle Brown, Mike Scales, Lane Traughber, Bill Clark, Richard Canaday, Joe Widner, Terry Patient.

1967 / Team Members

Bevin Aufrecht
Pete Bankson
Kim Brown
Merle Brown
Phil Brown
Richard Canaday
Randy Carr
Doug Hadden
Guy O'Bryan
Leon Pruett
Kirk Sunderland
Lane Traughber
Ken Weaver
Trent Wilcox
Assistant Coach: Bill Meyers

Dick Bowman
Bob Barnfield
Rick Hadden
Phil Daniels
Rex Harris
Gary Ross
Dan Robinson

1968 / Team Members

Pete Bankson
Randy Carr   Co-Capt.
Kirk Sunderland
Stein Villumstad Co-Captain
Joe Zeeb
Bevin Aufrecht
Lane Traughber
Mike Scales
Paul Gorden
Max White
Bill Ervin
Vince White
Dan Robinson

John Thomas
Tom Younker
Steve Canaday
Gary Ross
Rex Harris
Tom Ritter
Rob Buzan
Dale Usinger
Les Albert
Rodney Kraus
Dan Sutton
Jim Oglesby

1969 / Team Members

Scott Vanburen
Rex Harris
Tom Ritter   Co-Captain
Dan Robinson
Dan Sutton

Dale Usinger
Jeff Zeeb
Rodney Kraus
Greg Mathias
Kent Hadden

David Fitzgerald
Paul Gorden (Soph.)   Co-Captain
Greg Thiele
Ken Ervin
Dell McCoy
Brent Damery
Tom Younker
Phil Daniels

Bob Scrimpsher
Vince White
Bill Huffman
Kent Aufrecht
John Thomas
Les Albert
Max White

Freshman Relay Team Record Holders

Greg Thiele	49.4
Ken Ervin	49.4
Dell McCoy	49.4
Brent Damery	49.4

1970 / Team Members

Tom Ritter   Capt.
Dan Robinson
David Fitzgerald
Paul Gorden
Stan Henderson
Dale Usinger
Tom Younker
Dennis Younker
Jeff Zeeb
John Heller
Bill McPherson
Bruce Ervin

Greg Thiele
Dell McCoy
Richard Ritter
Greg Mathias
Mike Oxby
Kent Hadden
Brent Damery
Ken Ervin
Aaron Sunderland
John Allen
Frank Bailey
Kevin Nichols

1971 / Team Members

Les Albert
Paul Gorden   Capt., Top Scorer
Stan Henderson
Dale Usinger Capt.
Tom Younker
Brent Damery
George Meisenhelter
Greg Thiele
Dell McCoy   Capt.

Mike Oxby
Tim Armstrong
Jamie McNeely
Randy Damery
Bob Marler
Werner Liegel
John Allen
Mark Wolfer
Bob Brown

Kent Hadden
Greg Mathias
Ken Hackney
John Heller
Jeff Zeeb
Frank Bailey
Jim Bos
Dennis Younker
Aaron Sunderland
Rick Green
Doug Fitzgerald

Bruce Ervin
Don Damery
Jack Cater
Kevin Burns
Roger Miller
Ken Mercer
Richard Ritter
Duane Noland
Mark Aufrecht
Mike Kuehl

State Qualifiers

Paul Gorden	22.4	220 Yd. Dash

New Records

Paul Gorden	220 yd dash State Qualifier	22.4
Paul Gorden	180 yd. low hurdles	20.9
Dale Usinger	440 yd. dash	54.3
Jim Bos	2 Mile Run	10:44

880 Relay Team
Undefeated Against 35 Schools

Paul Gorden	880 Relay
Dale Usinger	880 Relay
Brent Damery	880 Relay
Ken Hackney	880 Relay

Statisticians: LaNeva Henderson, Janet Mercer, Pat Nolen, Michelle Nichols

1972 / Team Members

Brent Damery Co-Captain, Top Scorer
John Heller
Greg Mathias
George Meisenhelter
Dell McCoy

David Burns
Rodney Damery
Jack Cater
Steve Kraus
Tony Beckett

Greg Thiele
Jeff Zeeb
John Allen
Frank Bailey   Co-Captain
Jim Bos
Mark Wolfer
Dennis Younker
Kelly Chapman
Randy Damery
Doug Fitzgerald
Mike Oxby
Duane Noland

Ken Mercer
Dick Martin
Rodney Houser
Rick Sevits
Harold Kraus
Russell Frey
Randy Hammond
Barry Hammond
Brian Sheffield
David Pistorius
Tim Armstrong

New Records

Jim Bos	2 Mile Run
Frank Bailey	Mile Run
Brent Damery	440 Yd. Dash
Brent Damery	Discus

Statisticians: Pat Nolen, Michelle Nichols, LaNeva Henderson, Gerald Fairhall

1973 / Team Members

John Allen
Frank Bailey   Capt.
Bill Beck
Jim Bos
Luciano Frasca
Mark Wolfer
Dennis Younker
Tim Armstrong
Kevin Burns
Randy Damery
Doug Fitzgerald   Top Scorer
Ken Mercer
Duane Noland
David Pistorius
Steve Kraus

Tom Cater
Sam Robinson
Russell Frey
Tom Jones
Brent Carter
Ken Gilpin
Scott Armstrong
Dan Fitzgerald
Kent Kraus
David Burns
Tony Augustine
Sam Tucker
Russell Hobson
Rodney Damery

State Qualifier:

Doug Fitzgerald	100 Yd Dash	10.2

New Records

Jim Bos	2 Mile Run	10:20.3
Randy Damery	880 Yd. Run	2:03
Frank Bailey	Mile Run	4:32
Kelly Chapman	Long Jump	20'.5"
Doug Fitzgerald	100 Yd. Dash	10.2

Statisticians: Tina Beckett, Terri Logue, Debbie Drysdale, Cathy Meisenhelter

1974 / Team Members

Tim Armstrong MVP	Mike Bourisaw
Kevin Burns	Brent Carter
Randy Damery	Sam Tucker
Doug Fitzgerald Capt.	Ken Gilpin
Ken Mercer	Dave Clark
Duane Noland	Clyde Ross
Dan Byard	Brian Robinson
Rodney Damery	Randy Kraus
Russell Frey	Rick Scales
Steve Kraus	Dan Fitzgerald
Dick Martin	David Darnell
David Pistorius	Tony Augustine
Tom Cater	Scott Younger
Tom Jones	Ed Bailey
Tim Tucker	Jim Nolen
Tony Beckett	Harry Crump
Russ Hobson	Tim Rainey

State Qualifier

Doug Fitzgerald	100 Yd. Dash
	220 Yd. Dash

New Records

Doug Fitzgerald	100 Yd. Dash	9.9
Tim Armstrong	High Hurdles	16.0
Doug Fitzgerald	440 Relay	45.0
Randy Damery	440 Relay	45.0
Scott Armstrong	440 Relay	45.0
Duane Noland	440 Relay	45.0

Statisticians: Terri Logue, Cathy Meisenhelter, Debbie Drysdale, Tina Beckett

1975 / Team Members

Dan Byard	Sam Tucker
Rodney Damery	Gary Jackson
Russell Frey	Scott Younger
Steve Kraus	Brian Robinson
David Pistorius MVP, Top Scorer	Bill Behner
Scott Armstrong Capt.	Jim Nolen
Dan Fitzgerald	Ed Bailey
Ken Gilpin	Brad Eckols
Tom Jones	David Darnell
Tony Augustine	Dave Clark
David Scales	Kelly Armstrong
Harry Crump	Tom Dalluge
Dale Byard	Doug Woolever
Tim Rainey	Dick Martin

State Qualifers

Dick Martin	880 Yd. Run
Scott Armstrong	100 Yd. Dash
	220 Yd. Dash
David Pistorius	Long Jump
	Triple Jump

New Records

Dave Pistorius	Long Jump	21'10"
Dave Pistorius	Triple Jump	42'8"

Statisticians: Tami Clark, Teresa Brown. Terri Logue, Debi Clark

1976 / Team Members

Scott Armstrong   MVP, Top Scorer
Tony Augustine
Dan Fitzgerald
Ken Gilpin
Tom Jones
Chico Martorano
Sam Tucker
Ed Bailey
Harry Crump
David Darnell
Gary Jackson
Jim Nolen, Capt.
Brian Robinson
Scott Younger
Mark Houser

Kelly Armstrong
David Darnell
Scott Younger
Doug Collier
Todd Logue
Dale Byard
Jeff Canaday
Ed Bailey
Chris Blumenstein
Terre Moma
Doug Woolever
David Scales
Brad Eckols
Vernon Brandt

State Qualifiers

Scott Armstrong	100 Yd. Dash
	220 Yd. Dash
Jim Nolen	High Jump
Sam Tucker	Low Hurdles
Mark Houser	Triple Jump
David Scales	880 Yd. Run
Scott Armstrong	440 Relay
Dan Fitzgerald	440 Relay
Tom Jones	440 Relay
Brian Robinson	440 Relay
Scott Armstrong	880 Relay
Tom Dalluge	880 Relay
Tom Jones	880 Relay
Brian Robinson	880 Relay

New Records

Sam Tucker	High Hurdles	15.8
Jim Nolen	High Jump	6'2"
Scott Armstrong	100 Yd. Dash	9.9
	220 Yd. Dash	21.7

Dan Fitzgerald	440 Yd. Dash	53.8
David Scales	Mile Relay	3:40
Mike Jackson	Mile Relay	3:40
Sam Tucker	Mile Relay	3:40
Dan Fitzgerald	Mile Relay	3:40
Brad Eckols	2 Mile Relay	9:11.5
Bart Tucker	2 Mile Relay	9:11.5
Doug Collier	2 Mile Relay	9:11.5
Vernon Brandt	2 Mile Relay	9:11.5

Statisticians: Teresa Brown, Diana Virt, Tami Clark, Janice Drysdale

1977 / Team Members

Ed Bailey	Dan Binkley
Harry Crump	Doug Collier
David Darnell	Todd Logue
Mark Houser	Ben Tucker
Gary Jackson	Jim Brown
Terre Moma	Jeff Canaday
Jim Nolen	Bill Younger
Brian Robinson MVP	Larry Vaughn
Bart Tucker	Jeff Moma
Osamu Vemoto	Tod Nicholls
Scott Younger	Robert Myers
Kelly Armstrong	Dennis Noland
Dale Byard	Terry Simpson
Tom Dalluge	Rick Brown
Brad Eckols	Bruce Caudill
David Scales	Blake Sperry
Doug Woolever	Scott Walker
Mark Woodcock	Doug Mathias
Mike Jackson, Capt.	

State Qualifiers

Mark Houser	Triple Jump	43'9.5"	6th Place State Meet
Doug Collier	2 Mile Relay	7:59.6	3rd Place State Meet
David Scales	2 Mile Relay	7:59.6	3rd Place State Meet

| Bart Tucker | 2 Mile Relay | 7:59.6 | 3rd Place State Meet |
| Mike Jackson | 2 Mile Relay | 7:59.6 | 3rd Place State Meet |

New Records

Doug Collier	Mile Relay	3:29.5
Tom Dalluge	Mile Relay	3:29.5
Gary Jackson	Mile Relay	3:29.5
Mike Jackson	Mile Relay	3:29.5
Doug Collier	2 Mile Relay	7:59.6
David Scales	2 Mile Relay	7:59.6
Bart Tucker	2 Milee Relay	7.59.6
Mike Jackson	2 Mile Relay	7:59.6
Jim Nolan	High Jump	6'4"
Jeff Canaday	Discus	130'8.5"
Mark Houser	Triple Jump	43'9.5"
Doug Collier	Pole Vault	11'6" (tie)
Mike Jackson	440 Yd. Dash	52.3
Ed Bailey	2 Mile Run	10.9
Gary Jackson	High Hurdles	15.7

Statisticians: Rita Canaday, Marcelle Lewis, Kerry Miller, Cheryl Huffman, Carol Jackson

1978 / Team Members

Kelly Armstrong
Tom Dalluge
David Scales
Doug Woolever
Rick Brown
Doug Collier   Capt.
Mike Jackson MVP
Jeff Canaday
Steve Scales
Dennis Noland
Doug Mathias
Jerry King

Tod Nicholls
Mike Bonham
Steve Williams
Jim Brown
Ben Tucker
Bill Younger
Jeff Moma
Larry Vaughn
Scott Walker
Jeff Logue
Randy Revis
Craig Woolever

State Qualifiers

Mike Jackson	880 Yd. Run	**STATE CHAMPION**
	330 Low Hurdles	4th Place in State Meet
David Scales	880 Yd. Run	5th Place in State Meet
Doug Collier	440 Yd. Dash	
Bill Younger	Shot	
Rick Brown	Mile Relay	
David Scales	Mile Relay	
Doug Collier	Mile Relay	
Mike Jackson	Mile Relay	

New Records

Jeff Canady	Discus	135'6"
Bill Younger	Shot	51'1.25"
Rick Brown	Mile Relay	3:26.5
David Scales	Mile Relay	3:26.5
Doug Collier	Mile Relay	3:26.5
Mike Jackson	Mile Relay	3:26.5
Mike Jackson	440 Yd. Dash	50.3
	880 Yd. Run	1:54.24
	Low Hurdles	37.75
	High Hurdles	15.2

Statisticians: Melanie Ward, Marcelle Lewis, Carol Jackson, Cheryl Huffman, Andrea Robinson

1979 / Team Members

Rick Brown		Tom Younger
Jeff Canaday		Brett McPheron
Doug Collier	Capt.	Jerry King
Mike Jackson	MVP	Steve Williams
Todd Logue		Pat Walsh
Jeff Logue		Shannon Houser
Jim Brown		Larry Vaughn
Mike Bonham		Scott Woolever
Robert Myers		Randy Revis
Doug Mathias		Trent Logue
Jeff Moma		Steve Scales

Tod Nicholls
Dennis Noland
Ben Tucker

Bill Younger
Mike Weybright

State Qualifiers

Bill Younger	Shot
Doug Collier	440 Yd. Dash
Mike Jackson	Low Hurdles
Mike Jackson	880 Yd. Run **STATE CHAMPION**
Dennis Noland	Mile Relay
Todd Logue	Mile Relay
Doug Collier	Mile Relay
Mike Jackson	Mile Relay

New Records

Mike Jackson	High Hurdles	14.5
Mike Jackson	880 Yd. Run	1:53.57
Bill Younger	Shot	52'6.5"
Bill Younger	Discus	140'2"

Statisticians: Joanne Garner, Carol Jackson, Marcelle Lewis, Melanie Ward, Andrea Robinson

CROSS COUNTRY

Undeniably, the Blue Mound Knights were considered a basketball powerhouse in the Meridian Conference with Dick McDonald as their coach, but what some people may not remember is the phenomenal talent and versatility of the athletes produced during the McDonald era. McDonald began coaching Cross Country in the fall of 1971, and it wasn't long before the Knights had established themselves as the dominant force in the area. For 8 consecutive seasons from 1972 through 1979, the Knights were the Macon County Cross Country Champions. In his 9-year career as coach, McDonald collected 23 total championships which included mammoth events such as the Carlinville Invitational, which the Knights won 4 times. Additionally, McDonald's 1974, 1975, and 1979 cross country teams qualified for state. As an individual competitor, Mike Jackson placed 15th in state in 1977 and 21st in 1978.

Year	Championships
1971	
1972	Macon County
1973	Jacksonville Invitational
	Leroy Invitational
	Carlinville Invitational
	Macon County
1974	Carlinville Invitational
	Macon County
1975	Mt. Zion Invitational
	Effingham Invitational
	Macon County
1976	Mt. Zion Invitational
	Carlinville Invitational

	Jacksonville Invitational
	Macon County
1977	Carlinville Invitational
	Carlinville Fr./So.
	St. Joe Invitational
	Clinton Invitational
	Macon County
	District
1978	Macon County
	District
1979	Macon County

1st Cross Country Team 1971
Cross Country picture from the 1971
Blue Mound High School yearbook.

Row 1: Coach McDonald, Kent Hadden, John Heller, Dan Ryan, Dale Usinger, Werner Liegel, Brent Damery, Stan Henderson, Greg Mathias
Row 2: Dennis Younker, Tom Younker, Jim Bos, Mike Oxby, Randy Damery, Kevin Burns, Paul Gordon, Les Albert, Frank Bailey
Row 3: Greg Thiele, Richard Ritter, Mike Kuehl, Jack Cater, Donny Damery, Ken Mercer, Duane Noland, Tim Armstrong

Cross Country Teams
1971 – 1979

1971 (1st year as a sport at Blue Mound High School)
Team Members

Les Albert

Paul Gorden

Stan Henderson

Dale Usinger

Tom Younker

Kent Hadden

John Heller

Greg Mathias

Greg Thiele

Don Damery

Duane Noland

Dan Ryan

Brent Damery

Dennis Younker

Jim Bos

Mike Oxby

Randy Damery

Kevin Burns

Frank Bailey

Richard Ritter

Mike Kuell

Jack Cater

Ken Mercer

Tim Armstrong

Werner Liegel

Macon County Team:

Randy Damery

Jim Bos   Co-Captain

Frank Bailey   Co-Captain

Kevin Burns

Les Albert

Dale Usinger

Paul Gorden

1972
1st Place Macon County Meet
Team Members

Brent Damery

Gerard Fairhall

David Buchter

Frank Bailey   Co-Captain

Jim Bos   Co-Captain

Bob Marler

Don Damery

Jack Cater

David Burns

Tony Beckett

Mike Oxby
Dan Ryan
Werner Liegel
Dennis Younker
Mark Wolfer
Jamie McNeely
Dan Byard
Top Runners:
Jim Bos
Frank Bailey
Kevin Burns
Randy Damery
Mike Oxby
Mark Wolfer
Dennis Younker

Kevin Burns
Randy Damery
Mike Bourisaw
Steve Kraus
Ken Mercer
Tim Armstrong
Rodney Damery

1973
Team Members
First Ever State Qualifying Team

Frank Bailey
Bill Beck
Jim Bos
Luciano Frasca
Jamie McNeely
Mike Oxby
Richard Ritter
Mark Wolfer
Dennis Younker
Tim Armstrong
Kevin Burns
Randy Damery
Kevin Bafford

Tony Beckett
Ken Gilpin
Russ Frey
Steve Kraus
Mike Bourisaw
David Burns
Dick Martin
Dan Byard
Kent Kraus
Rodney Damery
Scott Armstrong

Top Runners
Mark Wolfer
Jim Bos
Frank Bailey
Mike Oxby

Kevin Burns
Dennis Younker
Randy Damery

Statistician: Terri Logue

1974
Team Members
Won the Macon County Meet
Qualified for Sectional

Tim Armstrong
Kevin Burns
Randy Damery
Tony Beckett
David Burns
Danny Byard
Rodney Damery
Steve Kraus
Dick Martin
Tim Rainey
Ken Gilpin

Tom Cater
Harry Crump
Sam Tucker
Terre Moma
Dan Fitzgerald
Brian Robinson
Jim Nolen
David Darnell
Kent Kraus
Scott Armstrong
Ed Bailey

Top Runners:
Tony Beckett
Rodney Damery
Ed Bailey
Kevin Burns
Tim Armstrong
Danny Byard
Randy Damery

Statisticians: Tina Beckett, Terri Logue
*also known as Mean Tina and Terrible Terri

1975

Team Members
Won Macon County Meet

Tony Beckett
Danny Byard
Russell Frey
Rodney Damery
Steve Kraus
David Pistorius
Scott Armstrong
Tony Augustine
Dan Fitzgerald
Kenny Gilpin
Sam Tucker
Dick Martin
Mark Weaver
Ed Bailey
Gary Jackson

David Clark
Tom Dalluge
Doug Woolever
Mark Woodcock
Harry Crump
Jim Nolen
David Darnell
Mark Beckett
Terre Moma
Brad Eckols
David Scales
Dale Byard
Tim Rainey
Kelly Armstrong
Brian Robinson

Top Runners:
Ed Bailey
Rodney Damery
Kelly Armstrong
Gary Jackson
Russ Frey
Sam Tucker
Tim Rainey
Tony Beckett
Tony Augustine
Brian Robinson

Statisticians: Teresa Brown, Terri Logue

1976
Team Members
Won Macon County Meet

Tim Allen

Tony Augustine

Dan Fitzgerald

Sam Tucker

Ed Bailey

David Darnell

Gary Jackson

Tim Rainey

Brian Robinson

Chris Blumenstein

Rick Brown

Roger Oxby

Bruce Caudill

Brad Eckols

Tom Dalluge

David Scales

Tim Rainey

Kelly Armstrong

Mike Jackson

Dale Byard

Todd Logue

Gary White

Top Runners:

Mike Jackson

Doug Collier

Ed Bailey

Kelly Armstrong

Brian Robinson

Sam Tucker

Gary Jackson

Tony Augustine

Dan Fitzgerald

Statistician: Teresa Brown

1977
Team Members
Won Macon County
Won 8 Team Trophies
Qualified for State

Ed Bailey

David Darnell

Mark Houser

Gary Jackson

Jim Nolen

Blake Sperry

Todd Brown

Dennis Noland

Scott Walker

Rick Brown

Tim Rainey
Brian Robinson
Bart Tucker
Kelly Armstrong
Dale Byard
Tom Dalluge
David Scales
Brad Eckols
Ben Tucker
Todd Logue

Doug Mathias
Bruce Caudill
Tod Nicholls
Jeff Moma
Bert Sturgis
Joe Crump
Mike Peer
Doug Collier
Mike Jackson
Jim Brown

Top Runners:
Mike Jackson
Doug Collier
Kelly Armstrong
Bart Tucker
Gary Jackson
David Scales
Ed Bailey
Tom Dalluge

Statisticians: Rita Canady, Kerry Miller

1978
Team Members
Won Macon County
Team placed 14th in the State Meet
Mike Jackson placed 15th in State

Kelly Armstrong
Dale Byard
Tom Dalluge
Brad Eckols
David Scales
Rick Brown
Doug Collier
Bruce Caudill
Mike Jackson
Todd Logue

Doug Mathias
Steve Williams
Todd Brown
Dennis Noland
Tod Nicholls
Scott Walker
Steve Miller
Steve Scales
Mike Weybright
Mike Stoutenborough

Robert Myers
Bill True
Jim Brown

Frank Shull
Ben Tucker
Bill Younger

Top Runners:
Mike Jackson
Doug Collier
Kelly Armstrong
Rick Brown
Robert Myers
Tom Dalluge
Bruce Caudill
David Scales

Statisticians: Rita Canady

1979
Team Members
Macon County Champs
Mike Jackson placed 21st in the State Meet
**Mike Jackson set the record on the BMHS course: 2.95 miles /
13.38 min.**

Rick Brown
Doug Collier
Mike Jackson
Todd Logue
Jim Brown
Joe Crump
Doug Mathias
Tod Nicholls
Dennis Noland
Ben Tucker
Mike Weybright
Shannon Houser
Craig Sperry

Mike Peer
Steve Williams
Bill Younger
Chris Usinger
Steve Miller
Duane Brown
Lanny Beckett
Bill True
Tim Baldwin
Marty McDonald
Pat Walsh
Scott Durbin

Top Runners:
Dennis Noland
Mike Weybright
Tod Nicholls
Doug Mathias
Doug Collier   Capt.
Mike Jackson   MVP
Rick Brown

Statisticians: Alice Smith, Jill Pistorius, Keri Wetzel (Inc.)

1977 Blue Mound High School Cross Country Team:
Rita Canaday, Mike Jackson, Kelly Armstrong, Bart Tucker, Gary Jackson,
Coach McDonald, David Scales, Ed Bailey, Doug Collier, Tom Dalluge,
Kerry Miller

Picture from the Blue Mound High School yearbook.

Won Macon County
Won 8 Team Trophies
Qualified for State

Senior Graduation Athletic Awards

1964	Bob Albers, Ron Naber, Alan Snyder
1965	Jerry Heller, Terry Rainey
1966	Paul Sperry
1967	Kim Brown
1968	Ken Huffman, John Pistorius
1969	Gail Edmunds
1970	Tom Ritter, Dan Robinson
1971	Dale Usinger, Tom Younger, Paul Gorden
1972	Brent Damery
1973	Frank Bailey
1974	Tim Armstrong
1975	David Pistorius
1976	Scott Armstrong, Kenny Gilpin
1977	Gary Jackson, Ed Bailey
1978	David Scales, Kelly Armstrong
1979	Mike Jackson, Doug Collier
1980	Bill Younger
1981	Steve Williams
1982	Trent Logue
1983	George Booker
1984	Mike Collier
1985	Did Not Coach
1986	Did Not Coach
1987	Did Not Coach
1988	Chad Jones
1989	Scott Jewsbury
1990	Eric Pistorius
1991	Jason Brown

PICTURES

Above: *Coach McDonald stands next to some of the Meridian Conference Gold Basketballs earned by Blue Mound teams. In 1984 the tournament directors decided to discontinue this particular trophy due to excessive cost. Coach McDonald motivated his undefeated team that year by promising them they would get a gold basketball trophy if they won the conference even if McDonald had to pay for it with his own money. In the end, the '84 team did win the conference and the Knights' Lettermen's Club voted to buy the prestigious gold ball trophy. This picture was taken at the Mounders' Museum in Blue Mound (Aug. 2012).*

Coach looking at old basketball uniforms on
display at the Mounders' Museum. Blue Mound's
colors were blue and white; however, the red trim
represented Boody Grade School, a school in
Blue Mound's district that closed in the 1970's.
Boody GS is also where Coach McDonald began his
career in 1961.

Coach McDonald being interviewed by Bruce Firchau
For the Hall of Fame Museum in Danville.

Coach McDonald in his old gymnasium.
The sign that bears his name is in the background.

From the *Decatur Herald and Review*.
The gym dedication Feb. 19, 1993
L to R: Tom Ritter, Phil Brown, Gary Jackson,
Tim Rainey, Kim Brown, Ed Bailey

The Early Days.
Photo released by the *Decatur Herald and Review.*

Liking what he sees, McDonald is pictured here
in a *Decatur Herald and Review* photo from February 1979.

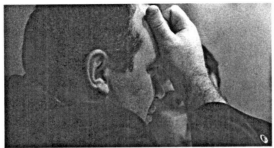

Coach McDonald in his early days. The caption on the back of the original read "Frustration." This picture was released b ythe Decatur Herald and Review.

All eyes are on Coach as he explains the game plan. Seated on the bench from left to right: Mark Houser, Gary Jackson, Brad Eckols, Ed Bailey, David Scales. Also tuning in with hands on knees: Todd Logue and Doug Collier.

Regional Champions: *Todd Logue, Coach McDonald, Gary Jackson, Mark Houser, Ed Bailey, Tim Rainey, Dave Scales, Tom Dalluge, Kelly Armstrong, Assistant Coach Phil Baca*

1970 / Coach McDonald's 1ˢᵗ Regional Championship Team
John Heller, Kent Hadden, Tom Ritter, Tom Younker, Dan Robinson,
Brent Damery, Dale Usinger, Stan Henderson, John Bonn, Paul Gorden

Surrounded by trophies, Coach McDonald speaks at
a sports awards banquet early in his career.

***The Knights directly after winning the Regional
Championship game against Assumption in 1983***
*Front Row: George Booker, Mike Collier, Brian Damery,
Chris Parsons, Mike Wilhoit, Bruce Bailey, Mgr. Todd Klay.
Back Row: Coach Baca, Eddie Morr, Eric Brown,
Pete Gilson, Brad Damery, Bob Koonce, Matt Sefried, Coach McDonald*

*Rolling along in the "Winning Streak" of 1977 – the
only Blue Mound team in history to go undefeated in
the regular season.*

2003 Alumni Tournament:
Front Row: Joe Crump, Gail Edmunds, Trent Logue, Doug Collier,
Coach, Brent Damery, Cory Lines
Back Row: Gary Jackson, Bill Younger, Dave Scales, Jeff Brown

1971 Cheerleaders: *Debbie Showalter, Linda Younker*
LaNeva Henderson, Lynette Botoner, Diane Noland,
Diane Lowe, Mascot / Marcy McDonald

1982 yearbook picture of the Blue Mound Knights Cheerleaders. Kneeling in front: Teresa Rhodemann; On hands and knees: Michelle Tucker, Annette Younker; Hands on knees: Marcy McDonald, Joanie Dillon; Pyramid L to R: Christie Sarver, LeAnn Thiele, Nikki Goad, Jill Wubben, Cheryl Morr

Basketball Statisticians 1983:
Kneeling: Tina Hite, Geri Sattler, Gretchen Damery
Middle Row: Erin Franklin, Tammy Brown
Standing: Sue Wubben, the Knight, Cheryl Drysdale

Coach Dick McDonald, center, with Blue Mound lettermen Doug Collier, Todd Logue, Mike Jackson, Bill Younger

Coach McDonald and players are pictured here in a photo from the *Decatur Herald and Review*. He appears to be in a jovial mood at practice. From the looks of it, Coach seems to jokingly have an issue with Bill Younger (far right) and looks to Mike Jackson for confirmation. Todd Logue (behind Coach) appears to offer his opinion, but Doug Collier (far left) is probably thinking, "I'm staying out of this." (Nov. 1978)

Pictured Left – Chris Parsons and Mike Collier were both 4-year starters for the Knights. They helped lead their team to Regional Championships in both 1983 and 1984. Parsons and Collier are both 1000+ point scorers. Pictures from the *Decatur Herald and Review*.

SPRINGFIELD SECTIONAL
TOURNAMENT·1970   10¢

SPRINGFIELD LANPHIER
BLUE MOUND
                    WINNER · GAME 1
                                    WINNER · TO PEORIA
                                    SUPERSECTIONAL
LINCOLN
DECATUR EISENHOWER
                    WINNER · GAME 2

Back in the 1960's and 70's, Blue Mound - a school of around 200 - often excelled to the point where its teams were paired against much larger schools. Pictured here is a sectional tournament program from 1970 showing Blue Mound playing Springfield Lanphier.

Dick McDonald

McDonald recuperates

Blue Mound High School Coach Dick McDonald remains in satisfactory condition in the cardiac care unit at St. Mary's Hospital after suffering a heart attack Tuesday afternoon.

"They (doctors) can't find any damage," said McDonald. "But I don't know how much longer I'll be here. I'm lying in bed strapped to a heart monitor and I'm limited to 1,200 calories a day."

"They haven't told me when I can resume coaching," McDonald added.

Phil Baca has taken over in McDonald's absense. Baca was at the helm Tuesday night when undefeated Blue Mound registered an eighth victory with a 81-56 romp over Raymond Lincolnwood. Blue Mound was idle Friday night.

This article appeared in the *Decatur Herald and Review* in 1984. After recuperating, my dad and the Knights finished out the season 26-2 and won the Regional Championship. He stepped down from coaching after that year and then returned in 1988.

My dad loves the fact that even after being out of coaching for 21 years, he is still known to many as "Coach." The "93" represents the year he was inducted into the Hall of Fame. My brother and his wife bought him the custom Blue Mound Knights plate frame.

The Fourth Quarter

- A Sampling of Support
- Timeline
- Coach McDonald Today

A Sampling of Support

I have mentioned many times throughout this book that my dad maintains a huge collection of notes, cards, letters, and other memorabilia from his coaching years. We have decided to share just a few of the many he received over the years.

Over his 22 year career, Coach McDonald awarded many Varsity Letters, and while he does not remember who received the first, he does recall who received the last in 1991. While going through his copious collection of letters and cards, Coach found this note from Chris Scott. It remains a bittersweet memory for him.

Dear Coach McDonald,

Thank you very much for the graduation gift. It has truly been a great honor to play for you, what, with being your last ever varsity letter winner and all. You are a great inspiration, and I will definitely stay in contact with you in the future.

Sincerely,
Christopher J. Scott
"Took"

Rev. Robert Clark of the First Christian Church of Blue Mound sent this letter to my dad after he and the Knights suffered their first and only loss in the 1977 season. The Knights ended their season 27 – 1, losing only to Mt. Pulaski in the Shelbyville Sectional finals.

First Christian Church

SIXTEENTH STREET AND WABASH AVENUE

P. O. Box 164
Mattoon, Illinois 61938

ROBERT C. CLARK, Pastor   Church Phone (217) 234-2928   Parsonage Phone 234-6922

March 7, 1977

Mr. Richard McDonald
Blue Mound High School
Blue Mound, Illinois 62513

Dear Dick:

Congratulations on a highly successful season!

A lot of people think that winning has to do with putting points on the scoreboard more than anything else. Personally, I feel it has to do with developing a strong and tenacious attitude and philosophy of life. That's why I liked what I saw in you and your boys during both games of the Shelbyville Sectional. Your acts of sportsmanship near the close and at the end of the Mt. Pulaski game were most commendable.

In my book, you are all winners because winners are gentlemen both on and off the basketball floor and I saw gentlemen there from Blue Mound last Friday night.

Please convey my congratulations to the team. I am exceedingly proud of all of you.

Sincerely,

Bob Clark

Robert C. Clark

RCC:nls

Throughout his years at Millikin University, Coach Joe Ramsey was a respected friend of my dad and a true Blue Mound Knight fan. His note speaks volumes regarding the real philosophy of Blue Mound basketball. My dad and his players were known for their discipline and class on and off the court. Although winning was one of my dad's favorite things, discipline and pride were probably more important overall.

Big Blue

MILLIKIN UNIVERSITY
Athletic Department
Decatur, Illinois 62522
Phone: 217/424-6344

February 9, 1977

Mr. Dick McDonald
Basketball Coach
Blue Mound High School
Blue Mound, Ill. 62513

Dear Dick:

Just a note to let you know I thought your team showed real class and discipline in the manner they handled Illiopolis' attempts to rough them up Monday night. A lesser group would surely have lost their cool.

I have really enjoyed watching the Knights in action these last four games and wish you the best as you move towards an undefeated regular season and the tournament trail.

Sincerely,

Joe Ramsey
Head Basketball Coach

JR:mk

COLLEGE CONFERENCE OF ILLINOIS AND WISCONSIN   •   N.C.A.A. DIV. III

This document was compliments of Sen. Duane Noland who grew up in Blue Mound and played on my dad's teams throughout high school. Duane won many awards and has remained a good friend of our family.

STATE OF ILLINOIS
EIGHTY-SEVENTH GENERAL ASSEMBLY
HOUSE OF REPRESENTATIVES

House Resolution No. 2648

Offered by Representative Noland

WHEREAS, The members of this body are honored to recognize significant milestones in the lives of the people of this State; and

WHEREAS, It has come to our attention that Dick McDonald of Blue Mound will be inducted into the Illinois Basketball Coaches Association Hall of Fame; and

WHEREAS, Dick McDonald coached a total of twenty-seven years, and he was varsity coach at Blue Mound High School for twenty-two of those years; and

WHEREAS, Over that period, his teams won 373 games and lost only 193, and his Meridian Conference record was 177-65; and

WHEREAS, His teams won six Macon County Championships, seven regional championships, and seven conference championships, including five Meridian Conference championships by the Blue Mound Knights; and

WHEREAS, The entire Blue Mound community is deservedly proud of Dick McDonald; therefore be it

RESOLVED, BY THE HOUSE OF REPRESENTATIVES OF THE EIGHTY-SEVENTH GENERAL ASSEMBLY OF THE STATE OF ILLINOIS, that we congratulate Coach Dick McDonald as he is inducted into the Illinois Basketball Coaches Association Hall of Fame; that we commend him for his dedication to the young people of this State; and that we extend to him our most sincere best wishes for the future; and be it further

RESOLVED, That a suitable copy of this preamble and resolution be presented to Dick McDonald as an expression of our respect and esteem.

Adopted by the House of Representatives on December 3, 1992.

Michael J. Madigan, Speaker of the House

John F. O'Brien, Clerk of the House

This congratulatory letter from Gail Edmunds (Class of 1969) is one of many Coach McDonald received after being inducted into the Illinois Basketball Association Hall of Fame in 1993. As with many of the letters he received, it appears Gail has some fond memories of his high school sports career. Coach McDonald particularly likes this letter because it came from the "early" days of his career, before he became a seasoned coach. He is thankful to know he had as much of an impact as a young coach as he did in the height of his career.

7541 Gannon Avenue
University City, MO 63130

June 1, 1993

Mr. Richard McDonald
Blue Mound High School
Blue Mound, Illinois 62513

Dear Coach,

I saw in the Blue Mound Leader the stories about your induction into the Illinois High School Basketball Hall of Fame and the renaming of the gym in your honor. Let me add my congratulations to you on these two achievements.

I look back with a great deal of pride to my high school basketball days. It was a lot of hours and work. It was also a lot of fun and a great way to impress the girls, two important considerations to a 16 year old. Do you remember my famous head fake and bubble butt rebounding technique?

My fondest memories are making the varsity squad the latter part of my sophomore year, holding Dale Grinestaff, the County Tournament MVP to 8 pts. my senior year, and persuading you to let us (me, Tom Yonker, Dale Usinger, Dan Robinson, Brent Damery, Tom Ritter, Dan Green, and Eric Thiele) play run and gun instead of pattern ball. That change in approach paid bigger dividends the next year. I'm also proud of being named captain by my teammates and winning the rebound award. You once told me that I was not the most talented player you ever coached, I think Paul Sperry probably was up to that point, but that I was as smart a player as you had ever coached.

I occasionally play a few hoops. I still don't have much spring but I still got the touch. Leave me open at 15 ft. and you can count it. My son is almost 4 and last Sat. we set up the goal outside. He doesn't look like he has much spring either but he goes to hoop well and likes to put 'em up. Now if he can just learn the head fake......

Best Wishes,

Gail Edmunds
Captain, Blue Mound Knights, 1969.

David Pistorius, Class of 1975, read this speech at the gym dedication in 1993. He and Coach McDonald had a special relationship in high school, and they have kept in touch over the years since.

Coach-it's an honor to be here in your name and in this school's name. You've touched all of us in some way and we have tremendous memories of our times together. In fact, I wrote down some of those memories and I've titled it.

WE REMEMBER...

-We remember the great times as well as the tough times.
-We remember the games--the Stonington's, Macon's, Mt. Zion's and the Bethany's, the Rochester's & Lanphier's, the Stew-Straw's & Pulaski's.
-We remember the long hours at Wise Park wondering if coach was watching us out his window.
-We remember the conditioning & the drills, along with the fast break down the side-line, the full-court press, the 3 quarter press, the half court trap, the zone defense with man to man influence, the 2-1-2, the 1-2-2, the forty-one and the famous trash.
-We remember the practices--oh do we remember.
-We remember the statics, the quarters and the 3 man weave--without the weave.
-We remember our stylish fashions--the blue slacks and shirts along with the white sweater vests.
-We remember the bus rides after a bitter loss or even a win which seemed like a loss, where you didn't even take a breath. We also remember those long quiet rides when it seemed like it took days to get back.
-We remember the perfection--spelled with a capital P.
-We remember the hair-cuts (isn't it interesting how things come back).
-We remember the psychology you used.
-We remember the clay pigeons and our names on them.
-We remember the firm hand and the strong, strong voice.
-We remember the trophies-The Meridian Conference Gold Basketballs, the Conference tourneys, the Macon County's, the Regionals and the Sectionals.
-We remember the butt chews and will never forget the follow-up pats on the back to re-affirm your affection for us.
-We remember the nick-names--Brownie, Younk, Noodles, Pit Beaver, Coma-Cozi, Snowbird, Arangatang, Hoss, Horse, Jack, Morris, Crazy Legs, Juice and my favorite--Bug-Hunter.
-We remember the hours of counseling-those one on one conversations.
-We remember the list that you carry in your billfold and look forward to that time we'll come together and reminisce.
-We remember your convictions and now we too live with those.
-We remember the excitement and the drama, the smiles and the tears.

Coach, thanks so much for the memories. We'll never forget the values you instilled in us. We remember those three little words you gave us so many times that we will treasure the rest of our lives--PRIDE, DEDICATION, AND DISCIPLINE. So here's to you coach--Congratulations on a fabulous career--we're proud to have been part of it!

Hoss "75"

In April of 2012, David Pistorius was inducted into the Illinois Basketball Hall of Fame. Celebrating with him at the ceremony was his family; high school and college teammate, Gary Jackson and his wife Janice; and Coach McDonald and his wife Ellen.

Jan 17, 1970

Dear Dick,

Congratulations on the County Championship. I listened to your game on the radio. I know how happy it made you. Convey my congratulations to the team. Good luck the rest of the way.

Yours truly,

Bob Miller

Coach McDonald has never forgotten his early years as an assistant coach under the direction of Coach Bob Miller. After Miller left to coach at Mattoon High School, he still kept in contact with McDonald.

McDonald Timeline

1939   Richard Lee "Dick" McDonald was born to Harold and Margaret (Wood)   McDonald.

1945   McDonald attends 1st grade at Prairie Hall Grade School one-room school house and stays at Prairie Hall through 5th grade.

1950   McDonald goes to Dalton City Grade School where there are organized sports for his 6th grade year and stays there through 8th grade.

1953   McDonald begins his freshman year at Mt. Zion High School.

1957   McDonald graduates from Mt. Zion High School.

1957   McDonald begins college at Illinois State Normal University. (fall)

1958   Illinois State Normal University changes its name to Illinois State University for McDonald's second year of attendance.

1961   McDonald graduates from Illinois State University. McDonald marries Ellen Bone of Oakley, Illinois. McDonald begins teaching science and coaching 5th – 8th grade baseball, 5th & 6th grade basketball, and assisting with the 7th & 8th grade basketball teams at Boody Grade School.

1962   McDonald adds 7th & 8th grade basketball and 5th – 8th grade track to his coaching   duties at Boody.

1963   McDonald begins teaching high school science and assumes guidance duties at Blue Mound High School. Coaching duties at Blue Mound include varsity baseball and junior varsity basketball under the direction on Coach Bob Miller.

1964   McDonald and his wife Ellen celebrate the birth of their son Martin Frank on August 3, 1964.

1966   McDonald becomes the varsity basketball coach of the Blue Mound Knights after Coach Bob Miller left Blue Mound to become Mattoon High School's head basketball coach. McDonald earns his Master's degree from Illinois State University. McDonald becomes the boys' track coach. McDonald and his wife celebrate the birth of their second child, Marcy Bess on March 2, 1966.

1967   McDonald retires from coaching baseball to focus on coaching running sports and basketball.

1971   McDonald begins coaching cross country. McDonald retires from coaching basketball after the 1971 – 72 season. McDonald is named *"Decatur Herald and Review* Track Coach of the Year."

1973   McDonald returns as head basketball coach of the Blue Mound Knights.

1976   McDonald is named *"Decatur Herald and Review* Track Coach of the Year."

1977   McDonald is named *"Decatur Herald and Review* Track Coach of the Year."

1979   McDonald is named the "Illinois Basketball Coaches' Association District 11 Coach of the Year." McDonald is chosen from approximately 90 schools as *"Decatur Herald and   Review* Area Coach of the Year." McDonald is named *"Decatur Herald and Review* Track Coach of the Year."

1980   McDonald retires from coaching track and cross country.

1984   McDonald retires from coaching basketball.

1988   McDonald returns as head basketball coach of the Blue Mound Knights.

1992   McDonald retires from coaching for the final time.

1993   The Blue Mound High School Gymnasium is dedicated to Coach McDonald at the last home basketball game before consolidation with Macon the following year. The gym is named "McDonald Gymnasium." (Feb. 19, 1993). Coach

McDonald is inducted into the Illinois Basketball Coaches' Association Hall of Fame on April 24, 1993.

2011   McDonald celebrates his 50th wedding anniversary with his wife Ellen. McDonald begins the process of nominating David Pistorius (Class of 1975) for the Illinois Basketball Players Hall of Fame.

2012   McDonald attends the Hall of Fame induction ceremony for David Pistorius in Bloomington, Illinois (April). McDonald begins the process of nominating Gary Jackson (Class of 1977) for the Illinois Basketball Players Association Hall of Fame (April) Coach McDonald is interviewed by David Firchau for the Illinois Basketball Hall of Fame Museum. McDonald's video and other Blue Mound Knights facts and memorabilia are on display at the museum in Danville (August).

Coach McDonald Today

Coach McDonald still lives in Blue Mound, IL, with his wife of 51 years, Ellen. Since leaving education and coaching, McDonald has helped his wife design and complete the total remodeling project of their 2-story home on Lewis Street. He is an avid vegetable gardener and also spends time helping Ellen maintain their lavish flower gardens.

Coach McDonald greatly enjoys spending time with family. He has 1 son, Martin "Marty," and 1 daughter, Marcy; a daughter-in-law, Kathy; son-in-law, Vince Bialeschki; and 2 granddaughters, Abby and Andrea Bialeschki. He enjoys spending family vacations with all of them down at the Lake of the Ozarks every summer.

Coach and his wife Ellen in their home in Blue Mound
Celebrating their 50th wedding anniversary in 2011.

McDonald and his family in 2011: Son-in-law,
Vince Bialeschki; daughter,   Marcy; wife, Ellen;
Coach; son, Marty; daughter-in-law, Kathy; and
granddaughters Andrea and Abby Bialeschki

Acknowledgements

Decatur Herald and Review
Blue Mound Memorial Library
Gary Jackson
Renee Bailey
JaniceWeathers
John Moma
Christopher Scott
Coach Bob Miller
David Firchau
David Pistorius
Duane Noland
Rev. Robert Clark
Joe Ramsey
Gail Edmunds
Renee Trimble
Alice Smith
Mike Martin
Gretchen Kirby

A Special Thank You

To Ellen McDonald
In the early years, my mom attended games, raised children, worked inside and outside the home, laundered basketball warm ups, and never complained about the long hours my dad spent at practices, games, and meets. Concerning this book, it was her organization of newspaper clippings, photos, and other memorabilia that moved this project along rather quickly. She was also extremely patient with us as we insisted on turning every family gathering for nearly a year into a chance to work on this book. Thank you, Mother. You are one special lady!
       Love,
       Dick and Marcy

CPSIA information can be obtained at www.ICGtesting.com
Printed in the USA
LVOW102140261112

308869LV00007BA/1065/P